Growing

as God's people

STUDENT WORKBOOK

Prepared by Noel E. Weiss for the
Board for Congregational Life,
Lutheran Church of Australia.

Lutheran Publishing House,
Adelaide, South Australia.

ISBN 0 85910 179 7

INTRODUCTORY LESSONS

1 CHAPTER

ALWAYS GROWING

God made you his own child through Holy Baptism. He made you a new person in Christ. Since then he has caused you to grow as his child. He wants you to keep on growing.

READ "GROWING..." pages 5-7.

Think about these questions:

Why is Baptism so important for you as a Christian?

Why can only God make you grow as one of his people?

Why does God want you to keep on growing?

What is his plan for you?

TIME FOR REFLECTION

We show that we are growing as God's people by being more and more faithful to God and his Word.

Here are some important things in your life. How can you show that you are one of God's people in each of these things? Write down what you think.

... how I feel about my confirmation lessons:

... how I feel about worshipping God:

... how I treat others:

... how I share in family life:

FOR DEVOTIONS

A Think about this saying:

"In every congregation you find two different kinds of people. I call them trees and posts. When you put in a tree it begins to grow. When you stick in a post it begins to rot. We pastors have a delightful time watching trees grow. But it is a sad business watching posts decay!" *(Dr. A.C. Dixon)*

What kind of people are meant by the "posts"?
What kind are meant by the "trees"?

READ Psalm 1. *How can God make you like a tree? How would you show that you are one of God's "trees"?*

2

B READ *Colossians 1:9-14.*

Paul prays for the Colossians (vs 9-12a) asking God to:
... help them grow in knowledge and understanding and in doing what pleases him;
... strengthen them in living as God's people.

Why is this important also for you? THINK about how you can grow as one of God's people.

God did great things for the Colossians, bringing them into the kingdom of Christ and setting them free from sin (vs 13-14).

How has God done this for you?

C PRAY *a short prayer:*

... thanking God for making you one of his people;
... asking him to help you grow as his child.

FAMILY TIME

TALK to your parents about why they think it is important for you to be confirmed. Conclude with a short devotion. You could read Colossians 1:9-12a, followed by your own prayer.

MORE TO DO

1. Find the six chief parts of Christian doctrine in this letter puzzle. (See "Growing.." page 7)

```
H L M C R K P G H O L Y B A P T I S M N B K
K M H C Z R T L P J G O B R E Q O L M N C L
L P H T O B C Z A O T F R K L Y V Z D F P I
J O H D C M N Q R P K J D D V F L P Y T W Q
T E N C O M M A N D M E N T S F O L P T Q W
V G S R M K L P G V Z Q U T Y P T O H L R Q
L J F E K M C F T P L T W R M X R C B V L P
D Y U E H B C R Y O P L F A W M K A B Y R Q
F P X D L P O I G C Z U T Y E Q U I Y L N C
M B C I Y E L P C V O F F I C E O F K E Y S
H O L Y C O M M U N I O N F Y P L M F D R L
```

2. Find the answers to complete the puzzle:

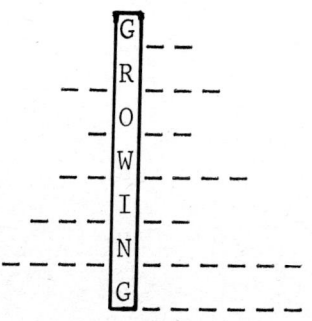

1. The Being who gives me life.
2. The Saviour who is my Lord.
3. God helps me grow through his ....
4. The nature God gives me through Baptism.
5. God makes me a member of his ......
6. God promises to give me ....
7. The aim of this confirmation course is to help me keep on ....

CHAPTER 2 — GOD'S POWERFUL WORD

God communicates with us through his Word. He speaks and works with us today through the Bible. This is his Word in writing.

READ "GROWING..." pages 9-11.

Think about these questions:

1. Why did God give us his Word?
2. Through which men did God give his Word?
3. What does it mean that God gave the Bible "by inspiration of the Holy Spirit"?

Write down what the Bible means to you:

TIME FOR REFLECTION

God's people treasure the Bible as God's way of speaking to them today. However, the following people don't think of the Bible in this way.

Write down what you could say to them to show your respect for God's Word.

1. Jack never reads his Bible. He says it is too old-fashioned.

2. When Dad asked Sue whether she read her Bible regularly, she replied, "Sometimes, but often I don't seem to get time".

3. When Bill saw Jim reading the Bible he told him he was wasting his time. "How do you know the Bible is true and not just fairy stories?" he asked.

FOR DEVOTIONS

A Henry M. Stanley set out in 1872 to find the missionary, Dr. Livingstone, who was lost in central Africa. He started his journey with 73 books, but travelling in the jungle was so hard that he couldn't keep carrying so many books. Gradually he threw them all away, day by day, until he had only one book left - the Bible. He read through his Bible three times during that amazing trip!

Why did Stanley keep his Bible?

READ John 8:32. THINK about how God will bless you as you faithfully study his Word.

B READ Psalm 119:97-105.

In this Psalm God's "law" is the old Testament Bible. The psalmwriter loves this Word of God. It is in his mind all the time and is sweet like honey to him.

How can you show that the Bible is precious to you?

The Word of God is most important for this psalmwriter because it gives him a true understanding of life, helps him follow God and know what is right.

How can the Bible be a light for your path?

C SAY a prayer, thanking God for giving you his Word and asking him to give you a love for the Bible.

FAMILY TIME

READ "God's Word at Work"(from "Growing...", p. 9) as a family devotion. Have the family talk about what God has done for them through his Word. Conclude with the Lord's Prayer.

MORE TO DO

Work out the crossword puzzle about the Bible.

CLUES:
ACROSS:

5. What God does when he speaks to us through his Word.
6. The Bible especially points us to this person.
8. The book that is God's Word in writing.
10. The men who wrote the Old Testament.

DOWN:

1. The New.... tells us the story of Jesus.
2. The men who wrote the New Testament.
3. The Person who inspired the Bible.
4. The special way God gave the Bible.
7. God gave us the Bible for our .....
9. Because God gave us the Bible it is .....

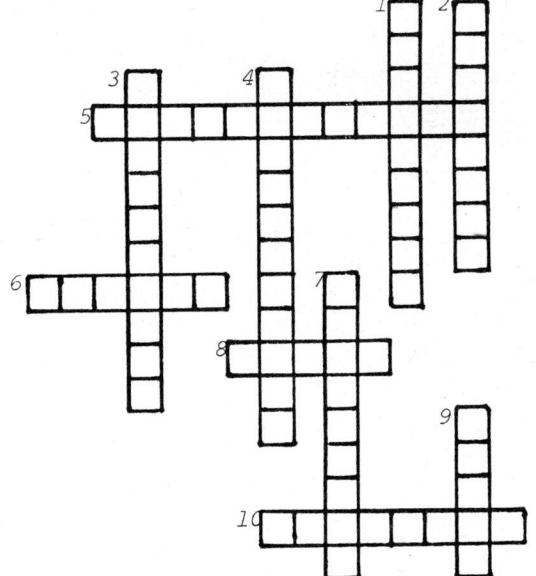

CHAPTER 3
LAW AND GOSPEL

The Law and the Gospel are two of the most important teachings in the Bible. The Law cannot save us from sins. It teaches us what kind of persons God expects us to be. It shows us that we are sinners who deserve punishment.

The Gospel is the good news that Jesus died for us so that we can be forgiven and be God's people. God is at work in our lives through the Law and Gospel each day.

READ "GROWING..." pages 13-15.

Think about what you have read and then complete these sentences:

1. To me the Law means

2. To me the Gospel means

3. I need to hear God's Law each day because

4. I need to hear the Gospel each day because

TIME FOR REFLECTION

The following people especially need to hear the Law or the Gospel. Tick the answer you think best, and put after it an L if it is Law and a G if it is Gospel.

a. Harry Brown never went to church. When his Christian friend invited him to a service he said he didn't need to go because he never did anyone any harm. His friend answered:

   ... "Not helping other people is just as bad as hurting them."
   ... "If you came to church you would hear the good news that God loves you."
   ... "In God's eyes all of us are sinners and need forgiveness."

b. As Scott was walking through a big department store he took a cassette and hid it in his pocket. When he boasted to his friend, Tom, about how easy it was, Tom replied:

   ... "If it's that easy, I'm going to try to get one too!"
   ... "That was stealing. I think it was wrong."
   ... "Weren't you scared of getting caught?"

c. Cathy pretended she wasn't a Christian because she was scared of being laughed at. Later she told her mother how ashamed she felt. Her mother said:

   ... "It was certainly a bad thing to do, Cathy. Next time why don't you speak up for Jesus?"
   ... "All of us let Jesus down sometimes. That's why we can be so glad he forgives us."
   ... "I certainly hope you'll never do that again!"

FOR DEVOTIONS

A When William Carey was asked why he preached the Law so severely to the Hindus in India, he replied; "I am like one finding his neighbour asleep with his house on fire. I make loud thumps to wake him so that he sees his danger and looks for escape."

READ Ezekiel 18:31-32. THINK about what God is saying to you here.
We cannot save ourselves by keeping the commandments.
Why?
Why did God give us the Law?

B Luther wrote; "The sweetness of the Gospel lies mostly in the little words: me, my, you. For example; 'Who loved ME and gave himself for ME'. 'Christ Jesus MY Lord.' 'Son, be of good cheer, your sins are forgiven YOU.' "

REPEAT 1 John 1:7 putting your name in the place of "us".
Why does the Gospel bring us such comfort and hope?

C READ Psalm 32:1-7.

When we don't listen to God's Law and try to hide our sins, it only hurts us. When we confess our sins and trust the Gospel God gives us the blessing of forgiveness.

Are you trying to hide any sins from God?
Open your heart to God and ask him for forgiveness.

FAMILY TIME

DISCUSS the section "Time for Reflection"(p.6) with your family.
READ Romans 6:20-23 and conclude by reading hymn 333.

MORE TO DO

Imagine St. Paul sent this urgent telegram. Decode it to get the message. (Clue: numbers stand for the letters of the alphabet.)

```
                     URGENT   TELEGRAM
TO: John Smith,

    20 1 11 5     3 1 18 5.    19 9 14    2 18 9 14 7 19    4 5 1 20 8.
    7 12 1 4     20 15     1 4 22 9 19 5    6 15 18 7 9 22 5 14 5 19 19
    1 14 4      5 20 5 18 14 1 12     12 9 6 5    3 15 13 5
    20 8 18 15 21 7 8    3 8 18 9 19 20.
                         25 15 21 18     6 18 9 5 14 4,
                                                    Paul.
```

Send a telegram to a friend telling him the Gospel in no more than 15 words....

UNIT ONE: THE TEN COMMANDMENTS

CHAPTER 4

GOD GIVES US HIS LAW

God, our loving Lord, has set down his will for us in the Ten Commandments. He has the right to give us his commandments, and demands that we keep them.

God gives the commandments to keep good order in the world, to show us how greatly we need the Saviour because we break God's Law, and to teach us how to lead lives that please him.

READ "GROWING..." pages 21-23

Decide whether these sentences are true or false:

1. ... God's commandments are concerned with our relationship to him and other people.
2. ... God first wrote out the commandments for Adam and Eve.
3. ... People can know God's commandments perfectly because they are written in their hearts.
4. ... Sinners should not be expected to keep the commandments perfectly.
5. ... The commandments serve as a fence, a mirror, and a guide for God's people.
6. ... Because we break God's commandments our only hope of being saved is through Jesus.

TIME FOR REFLECTION

The Law has three uses. *How is it being used in these cases?*

a. Sandra got angry with Anne and said mean, untrue things about her. Later, when she remembered the Eighth Commandment, she felt badly about what she had done and asked Jesus to forgive her.

b. The boys invited Alan to join them in stealing some apples, but Alan refused because he knew that this was against God's will.

c. Bert was speeding through the town on his motor bike. In the distance he saw a police car, so he slowed down.

FOR DEVOTIONS

A Here is a simple story. See if you can discover a deeper meaning.

Ferdie was a prize young bull. He liked to run around his paddock and show off to the cows. But he didn't like fences! "It would be so good to get outside and be free," he thought.

So, one day he got angry, pushed down the fence, and got out. He was free! He ran around bellowing to celebrate - straight into the path of a big transport, which he didn't see, coming down the highway. And that was the end of Ferdie!

What is the meaning of the story for you?

READ Psalm 119:33-35. Why are God's commandments good for us?
Why do Christians want to keep God's laws?

B   READ 1 Corinthians 13:1-7, Paul's wonderful hymn of love.

If we could love God and other people perfectly we would keep all the commandments. To love perfectly - that is the great demand God places on us.

Think about what is involved in having to love everyone.

This is a demand we can't meet. How thankful we can be that Jesus has paid this debt for us. God freely forgives us our lack of love. Now we are free, as his people, to love as much as we can - out of love for our Saviour.

Think of some practical ways you can show love to others today...

C   In a prayer ... thank Jesus for - loving you and all other people perfectly,
                                    - forgiving your sins and lack of love,
         ... ask him to give you a loving heart.

FAMILY TIME

TALK with your parents about rules which are important in your home. Discuss the need for these rules and why members of the family keep them.

READ Psalm 119:33-35 and pray, asking God for forgiveness and help to keep his commandments.

MORE TO DO

Unscramble the commandments and put them in the right order:

on hreot gsod : dsGo uoohrn mnea : ilkl od tno : tvoce otn od : spiworh dGo :

erup eb : ton do eatls : ntsrpae nuoroh : iel od nto :

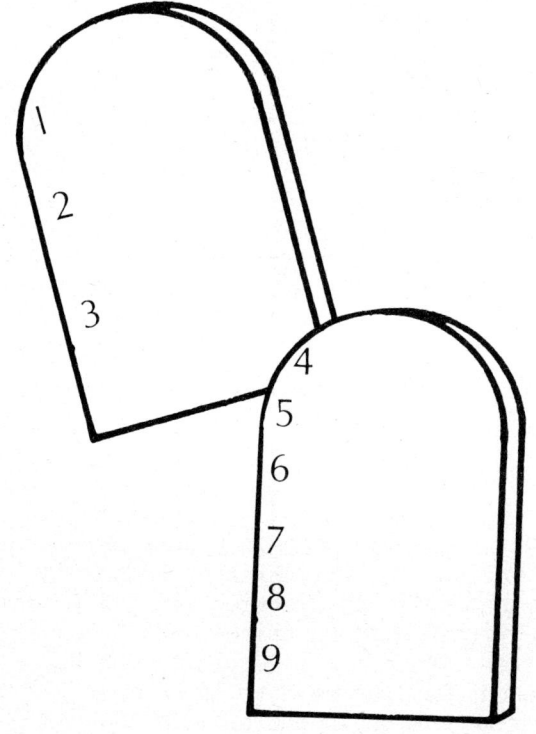

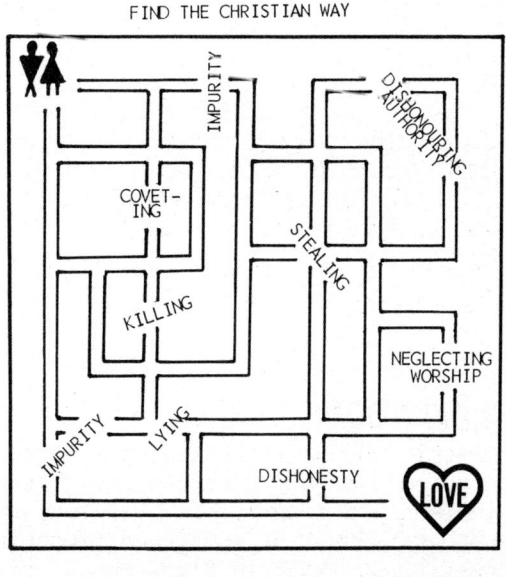

FIND THE CHRISTIAN WAY

CHAPTER 5
WITH ALL YOUR HEART

The true God, Father, Son and Holy Spirit, is our God. There is no other God beside him. All other so-called gods are idols and worshipping them is idolatry.

God wants to be the centre of our lives so that we fear, love, and trust him above anything else.

READ "GROWING..." pages 25-27. THINK about the following questions:

1. What does it mean to "have a god"?
2. How can you show that God is the centre of your life?
3. What might become more important than God in your life?

TIME FOR REFLECTION
JACQUIE'S DISAPPOINTMENT.

It was a happy day for the Edwards family when they moved into their new home. It was a fine home. Jacquie was especially pleased because at last she had a room of her own and a place for all her own things. She was quite proud of her new room.

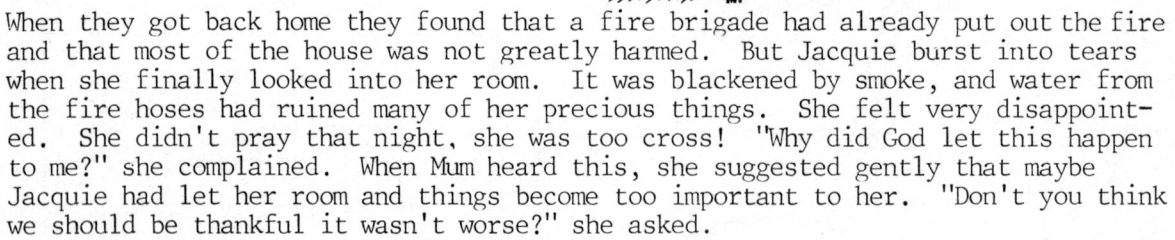

One day, when the family was out visiting, Dad got an urgent message; "Come home straight away. Your house is on fire!" You can imagine how worried they all were.

When they got back home they found that a fire brigade had already put out the fire and that most of the house was not greatly harmed. But Jacquie burst into tears when she finally looked into her room. It was blackened by smoke, and water from the fire hoses had ruined many of her precious things. She felt very disappointed. She didn't pray that night, she was too cross! "Why did God let this happen to me?" she complained. When Mum heard this, she suggested gently that maybe Jacquie had let her room and things become too important to her. "Don't you think we should be thankful it wasn't worse?" she asked.

How would you feel if you were Jacquie?
Write down what the First Commandment could teach Jacquie about her experience.

FOR DEVOTIONS

A Dietrich Bonhoeffer died as a martyr in 1945. He was a German pastor who opposed the teachings and policies of the Nazis. The Nazis feared Bonhoeffer's influence and work. In 1943 they put him into prison. Dietrich refused to give up his faith. He continued preaching and writing even in prison. On Sunday, April 8th, 1945, in Flossenburg prison, after conducting a service, Bonhoeffer was taken away to be hanged. As he was taken away, he said to Payne Best, an English prisoner, "This is the end, but for me the beginning of life".

READ Revelation 2:10.

THINK about ... how Bonhoeffer showed that he feared, loved, and trusted God above everything else,
... the meaning of this text for you.

B READ Psalm 115:1-11.

The psalmwriter worships the true God and praises him for his greatness and for his blessings. He shows how foolish it is for anyone to trust in an idol. People today don't usually make idols of wood or stone to worship, but they follow many false gods.

THINK about what it means for you in your daily life to fear, love, and trust in God above anything else.

C PRAY the following prayer. It would be good to learn it by heart.

O Triune God, Father, Son and Holy Spirit, you are my God and I belong to you. Help me to fear, love, and trust in you above anything else. In Jesus' name I pray. Amen.

FAMILY TIME

READ Psalm 115:1-11.

DISCUSS with your family the statement, "Most people in our country worship idols". Close with the prayer suggested above.

MORE TO DO

Find the text from page 27 of "Growing..." which would apply to these people:

a. Mrs. Jones gave up going to church after her son died.   ....

b. Andy prayed to God when he got sick. But he stopped praying when he didn't get better straight away.   ....

c. Father Damien was so filled with the love of God that he went to work in a leper colony.   ....

Use the international Morse code to read this Bible message.

```
A .-      N -.
B -...    O ---
C -.-.    P .--.
D -..     Q --.-
E .       R .-.
F ..-.    S ...
G --.     T -
H ....    U ..-
I ..      V ...-
J .---    W .--
K -.-     X -..-
L .-..    Y -.--
M --      Z --..
```

11

CHAPTER 6 — KEEP GOD'S NAME HOLY

God's name stands for God himself, for all that he is and all that he does. His name is to be kept holy. Out of fear and love for God we are to avoid all that dishonours his name and are to use it to honour and glorify him.

READ "GROWING..." pages 29-30.
THINK about these questions:

1. God tells you his name in the Scriptures. How does this make it possible for you to know him and be his friend?
2. How are you likely to take God's name in vain?
3. How can you use God's name in ways that honour him?

TIME FOR REFLECTION

The Second Commandment lists various ways we might take God's name in vain. DECIDE how the following people are using God's name wrongly. WRITE in your answers.

a. When a black cat ran in front of old Mrs. Gilbert, she mumbled some Bible verses to make sure no harm would come to her.
....

b. A member of a religious sect knocked on the door of Mrs. Kelly's home and began to speak to her. "Surely you don't believe that Jesus is truly God?" he asked. "The Bible shows plainly that that's not true!"
....

c. Mr. Clarke had a grocery. Quite often he cheated with his prices. He attended church regularly, however, because he thought it would help his business.
....

d. It was summer time. Stan was working hard digging the garden. "By God, it's hot today," he complained.
....

e. Tony was playing football. Once when he was going for the ball another player bumped him hard but fairly, and he fell down and hurt his knee. "Damn you!" he said.
....

FOR DEVOTIONS

A Everything that tells us about God in the Bible is really his name. But God has many particular names by which we know him.

A Bible scholar once tried to count the names of God in the Bible. He was amazed at how many he found. There were hundreds! He discovered that there were 208 names for Jesus alone in the Bible, and that the name of Jesus occurs 700 times in the New Testament.

As we come to know our loving God we praise him, using his beautiful names, which help us relate to him and to be his personal friend.

THINK about some names of God that you know and use them to praise him.

READ Psalm 148. The psalmwriter calls on all things to join in praise of God.

THINK about different ways in which YOU can praise God.

B Pastor Mentzer had many troubles. One bad thing after another seemed to happen to him. Then in 1704 he had to flee for his life when his house burnt down. He lost all his possessions.
"The devil shall not get the better of me and make me sad and discouraged," he said. Then he sat down and wrote this beautiful hymn (Lutheran Hymnal 446):

> O that I had a thousand voices
>   To praise my God with thousand tongues!
> My heart, which in the Lord rejoices,
>   Would then proclaim in grateful songs
> To all, wherever I might be,
> What great things God has done for me.

READ through this hymn. Notice how Mentzer praises God in the same way as the psalmwriter.

C WRITE a sentence thanking God for what he has done for you.

FAMILY TIME

Perhaps the family could make a list of things for which they can praise and thank God. Or they could each say a brief "thank you" to God for one of his gifts. Psalm 148 could be read and you could conclude with your own prayer of praise.

MORE TO DO

PSALM 116:17: "I will offer to thee the sacrifice of thanksgiving and call on the name of the Lord". Fit the words of the psalm into the puzzle.

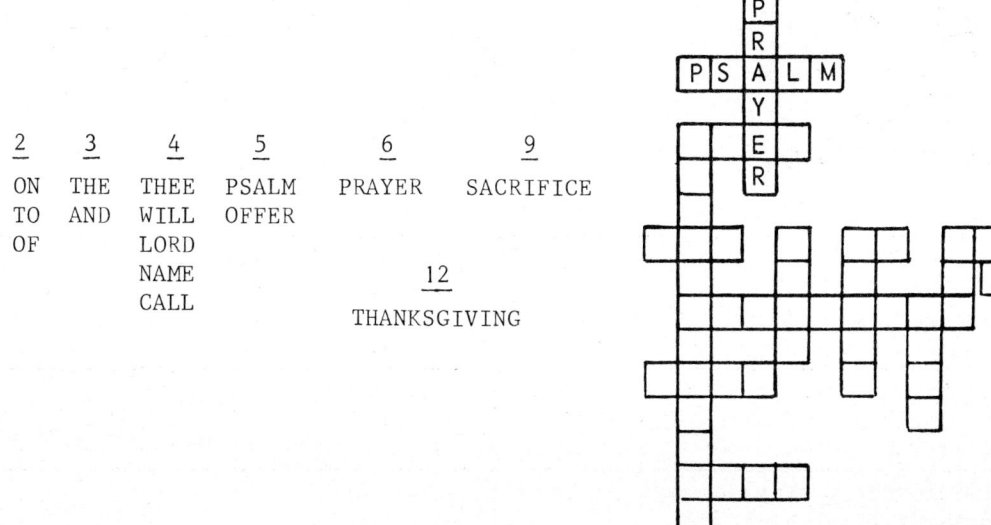

2	3	4	5	6	9
ON	THE	THEE	PSALM	PRAYER	SACRIFICE
TO	AND	WILL	OFFER		
OF		LORD			
		NAME		12	
		CALL		THANKSGIVING	

CHAPTER 7

WORSHIPPING OUR GOD

As God's people we worship him; we give him honour, thanks, and praise. God wants all people to worship him. We are gladly to hear and learn his Word, in our daily lives and together with the congregation on Sundays, and at other church festivals. God gives us his grace and blessings as we use his Word and Sacraments.

READ "GROWING..." pages 33-35.

Think about these questions:

1. Why does our worship begin with God?
2. Why does the congregation worship God on Sundays and other church festivals?
3. How do you break and keep this commandment? To find out, fill in the blank spaces with the right words.

God does not want us to _____ or _____ his Word or the _____. We are to _____ God regularly in our _____ ____ and in our _____. We do this by _____ public worship, by listening _____ to God's Word, by gladly _____ it, and by receiving the _____ _____ often. God also wants us to _____ the preaching of his Word.

```
Lord's Supper    neglect      private life
congregation     studying     sacraments
    despise      support      carefully
                 attending    worship
```

TIME FOR REFLECTION

WRITE IN how these people should feel about worshipping God.

	It would be better if:
a. Glenda usually day-dreams through the sermon because she doesn't think it is important for her.	Glenda
b. Ralph hardly ever goes to church. "You shouldn't go unless you feel like it," he says.	Ralph
c. Charlie doesn't pray any more because he doesn't think it helps.	Charlie

14

FOR DEVOTIONS

A Toyohiko Kagawa was born into a rich Japanese family and was brought up a heathen. Through the Gospel, Toyohiko became a Christian. His parents were angry that he had become a follower of Jesus. "You can't be in our family or share in any of our money if you worship the Christian God," they warned him. But worshipping God was the most important thing to Toyohiko. "There is nothing so important in my life as having God's Word and praising him," he decided. When he kept on worshipping God and studied to be a pastor, his parents turned him out.

God used Pastor Kagawa to preach to many Japanese and to lead them in worship. The joy of worshipping God was more important to him than money or even his family.

READ Psalm 100. THINK about how worshipping God can make you feel glad and happy.

B REPEAT the memory verse Luke 11:28. MAKE a list of blessings that come to you through worship.
Ask God to forgive you for breaking this commandment all the time.

C TAKE NOTE this week of the different times and places you worship God. Share this with your class.

FAMILY TIME

The family could TALK about different forms of worship they have experienced and why worship as a family is important.
You could READ "Why Do We Worship God?" (page 33 "Growing..."). Close by reading Psalm 100 and a prayer.

MORE TO DO

CLUES:

Down:
1. How we are to hear and learn God's Word
2. An attitude to God's Word which breaks this commandment.
3. The Third Commandment is part of this law. (see "Growing..." p.36)
4. The person who kept this commandment for us.
7. Special days, besides Sundays, when the congregation worships.
8. The solemn agreement God made with the Jews.

Across:
5. The festival which reminds Christians of Jesus' resurrection.
6. How God wants us to worship him.
9. One of the ACTS of worship.
10. What moves us to worship God.
11. The day on which the Jews worshipped.
12. What the word "worship" means.

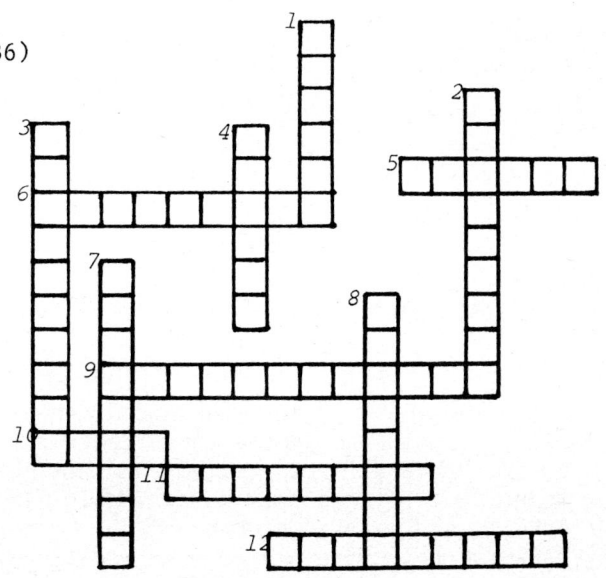

CHAPTER 8 — THOSE IN AUTHORITY

God commands us to keep the last seven commandments by loving our neighbour as ourselves. He places people in authority over us, like our parents. We are to honour, respect, and obey them as God's representatives.

READ "GROWING..." pages 37-39

COMPLETE these sentences:

1. Loving our neighbour means

2. Children are not to despise their parents by

3. Children honour their parents by

TIME FOR REFLECTION

There was trouble in the Green family. When Dad came home he discovered that someone had used his good tools in the shed and had left them lying all over the place.

"Did you do that?" he angrily asked Jim who was 6 years old.

"No!" said Jim quickly, "but I saw John in the shed." So Dad stormed off to John's room. "Go and put away those tools this instant!" he demanded.

John was upset at this. He hadn't touched the tools. When he didn't say anything or go straight away, Dad gave him a rough push and said, "Now get going!" John felt angry. Why was his dad treating him like this? He quickly went outside - but he didn't go to the shed. He went straight over to his friend's place.

When Mum got home from shopping, Jim owned up that he had used Dad's tools. He was sorry he had got John into trouble. Mum brought John back home and the family had a talk together. They all felt a bit uncomfortable. Then Dad told John he was sorry for making a mistake and yelling at him. "I shouldn't have done it," he said as he gave John a hug. "But you should still have done what Dad asked," Mum said.

The family was friends again, but Jim had to clean up the whole garage so that he would realize the wrong he had done.

Should John have done what his father told him? READ Ephesians 6:1-4 to help you decide.
Why is forgiving each other so important in our family life?

FOR DEVOTIONS

A READ Proverbs 3:1-4 and then think about this story.

As a young man, George Washington, the first President of the USA, had set his heart on going to sea as an officer in the British Navy. He had his kit on board a ship all ready to go when his mother sent a message saying he was not to go, but to come back home. Sadly George obeyed his mother and went back to school, and maths, which he hated! His mother was very pleased with him. "Always obey those placed over you, George, and God will bless you!"

God had great plans for George. He grew up to be the famous general who led his country to independence. If he had disobeyed his mother he never would have become the first President of the USA.

Obeying those God places over us often seems hard, but why does it bring great blessings?

B   "Unless children learn to obey in the home, a city, country or kingdom cannot be ruled properly. The home is the first government from which all other government comes. If the root of a tree is bad, then you can't get good fruit."
(Martin Luther)

REPEAT Colossians 3:20 and think about what Luther wrote.

Why does obeying parents please the Lord?
Often we don't honour and obey our parents or others placed over us as we ought. Why is this a sin against God? What do we deserve for our sins? Why can we be sure God forgives us these sins?

C   MAKE A LIST of your chief duties towards those in authority, referring to parents, your school teachers, the government.

FAMILY TIME

You could read the Family Code to the family (see below) and have them discuss it. Perhaps others in your home might like to help you make a poster setting out this code with pictures. You could hang it up on the wall near the meal table.

READ Ephesians 6:1-4 and then discuss the story and questions under "Time for Reflection" above.

MORE TO DO

Work out this Family Code by unscrambling the words:

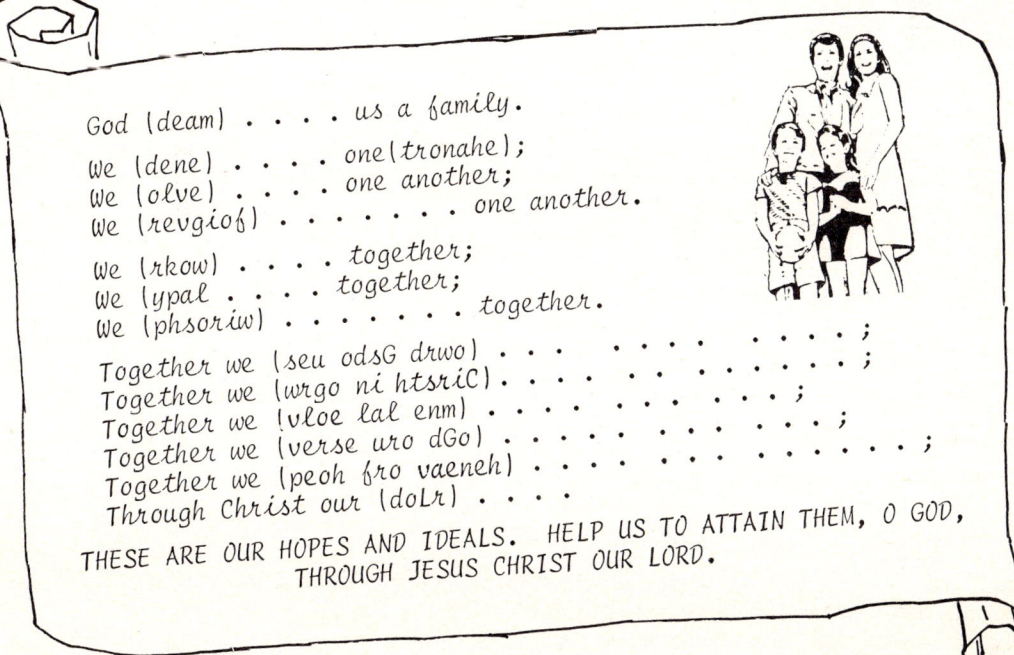

God (deam) . . . . us a family.
We (dene) . . . . one (tronahe);
We (olve) . . . . one another;
We (revgiof) . . . . one another.

We (rkow) . . . . together;
We (ypal) . . . . together;
We (phsoriw) . . . . together.

Together we (seu odsG drwo) . . . ;
Together we (wrgo ni htsriC) . . . . ;
Together we (vloe lal enm) . . . . . ;
Together we (verse uro dGo) . . . . . ;
Together we (peoh fro vaeneh) . . . .
Through Christ our (doLr) . . . .

THESE ARE OUR HOPES AND IDEALS. HELP US TO ATTAIN THEM, O GOD, THROUGH JESUS CHRIST OUR LORD.

9 CHAPTER — GOD'S GIFT OF LIFE

God protects the life he has given. He commands us not to do, think, or say, anything which will hurt or harm the bodily life of ourselves or other people. He wants us to show love to others by helping them in their physical needs.

READ "GROWING..." pages 41-43

THINK ABOUT:

What does it mean that God has authority over life?

In what ways does God protect our earthly life?

READ Mark 6:34-56.
Find three different ways in which Jesus cared for the physical needs of others. Then list three things you could do.

JESUS	I CAN
1.	
2.	
3.	

TIME FOR REFLECTION

CONNECT the right endings to the sentences. TICK the people who show a God-pleasing attitude.

a. Harry saw Norm fall off his bike but he didn't stop to help...

b. Harry sprained his ankle playing sport. Norm felt pleased...

c. Howard rides his motor bike recklessly through the town...

d. When a tramp asked Margaret for help she gave him a sandwich...

e. Jill visited her friend in hospital even though it meant missing a netball match...

f. Chris gave some of his pocket money to help refugees...

... because he is proud of how fast it will go.

... because she knew her friend would appreciate it.

... because they greatly need our help, he thought.

... "I'm in too much of a hurry to stop," he thought.

... "It's serves him right. He wouldn't help me," he thought

... "We should help someone in trouble," she said.

FOR DEVOTIONS

A READ 1 John 3:11-18. THINK about -

... how you might sin against this commandment by having hateful thoughts about certain people;

... how you can show your love for particular people by helping them in their physical needs.

B Two men, members of different African tribes, hated each other greatly, and were always looking for revenge. One of the men came across his enemy's daughter picking berries in the jungle. He grabbed hold of her and cruelly cut off both her hands. "Now I am revenged," he said.

Many years passed by. The young girl became a woman. One day an old, wretched, beggar covered in sores, came to her door, asking for help. Immediately she recognized him as the enemy who had cut off her hands. She sent her servant quickly to bring as much food as the poor wretch could eat. She watched him eat hungrily. When he was satisfied, she dropped the cloth which covered the stumps of her arms and said to him, "Now I am revenged".

What did she mean?
READ Romans 12:19-21.
Why is it so hard not to bear grudges? How can God help us to be kind and forgiving even to those who harm us?

ASK God to forgive you for bearing grudges, to give you a loving heart and to help you trust his forgiveness.

C During this week note one example of how you -
   a) break this commandment,
   b) help others in physical need.

FAMILY TIME

READ *1 John 3:11-18 and talk about* people in your community who are in need. (You may be able to find out about needy people from your pastor, your school, or social workers.)

DISCUSS with your family rules for healthy living.

MORE TO DO

Proper care of your body is important.

Fill out this chart.

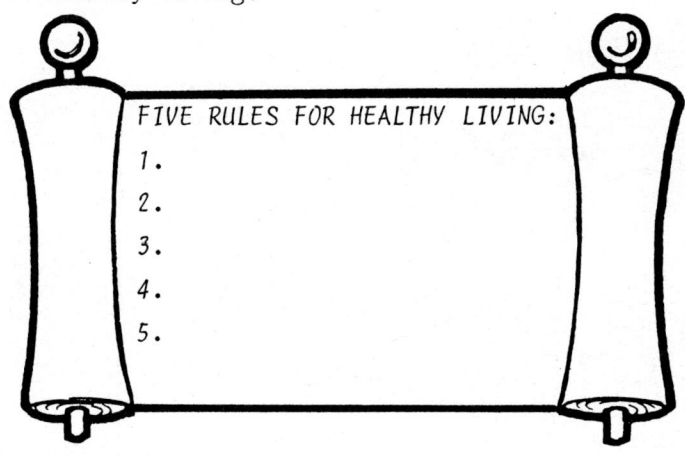

FIVE RULES FOR HEALTHY LIVING:
1.
2.
3.
4.
5.

```
A *      I :      S ▫      Use the symbols to decode the message:
C -      L +      T △
D ..     M ∽      U ⊣
E /      N \      V ⊥
F #      O x      W ⁒
G =      P ⊢      Y ⊙
H o      R ℵ
```

CHAPTER 10 — CREATED MALE AND FEMALE

God made us male and female. Sex is one of his good gifts and is to be regarded as sacred. God commands us all to be pure and decent in our thoughts, words, and deeds. Marriage is his institution and he reserves the full expression of sex for married partners. They are to love and be faithful to each other.

READ "GROWING..." pages 45-47

COMPLETE the sentences:

1. Sex is a good gift from God, but, because of sin, it can easily get ....

2. God wants us to live a .... life.

3. It is a hard.......... for a Christian to be pure, because of his enemies, ..., ..., and his ....

4. God helps us to be pure through ....

5. Marriage is God's ....

6. God wants married people to be ....

TIME FOR REFLECTION

How are these people being tempted to be impure?	How can you learn from the attitude of these people?
1. One of Gordon's friends gave him some sexy magazines.	1. In her devotions at night, Kathleen regularly asked God to help her be pure.
2. Ken started going with some boys who liked to tell filthy stories.	2. Mary dressed sensibly because she didn't like to show herself off.
3. Susan was asked out for a date to an R-rated movie by a boy with a bad reputation.	3. When David is troubled with sexy thoughts he tries to forget them by doing some work.
4. Alan went to a party where the young people began drinking heavily.	4. Grace said "No" when her boyfriend wanted to start some heavy petting.

FOR DEVOTIONS

A A visitor to a coal mine noticed some flowers growing at the mouth of the mine. They were blackened by coal dust. "Look how those flowers are ruined!" he told his wife. A miner who overheard, picked one of the flowers and shook it gently. At once the dirt fell off and left the beautiful petals shining white. "You see," said the miner, "the flower could grow here in all this dirt and not really be dirty."

READ Psalm 119:9-11.
Why is immorality like dirt?
How does God's Word help us to stay pure?

B Young people sometimes feel very guilty about sins of sex.
READ 1 John 1:7-9. THINK about how Jesus your Saviour removes your guilt and assures you of forgiveness.

WRITE a short prayer ...thanking God for forgiving you through Christ;
... asking him to help you to be pure.

C "You can't stop the birds flying over your head, but you can stop them making nests in your hair." (Martin Luther)

What did Luther mean?

READ Luke 6:43-45. THINK about how these words of Jesus relate to matters of sex.

FAMILY TIME

You could READ the story about the flowers at the mine and ask your family what they think it teaches Christians. Then READ Ephesians 5:1-8. Conclude with your own prayer.

MORE TO DO

Unscramble the words and put them in the proper place:

God helps us to be pure in various ways. He gives us his .... which helps us know and do his will. As we talk to him in .... he strengthens us. Keeping ourselves busy with useful .... and .... helps us overcome temptation. It is important for us to choose .... and to avoid ....

(bohibes   live cplesa   yperar   dwro   stihrcnai dnesfir   kwro)

We need clean 👂 👄 👁 ♡ to live a pure life.

Put the symbols where you think they fit best.

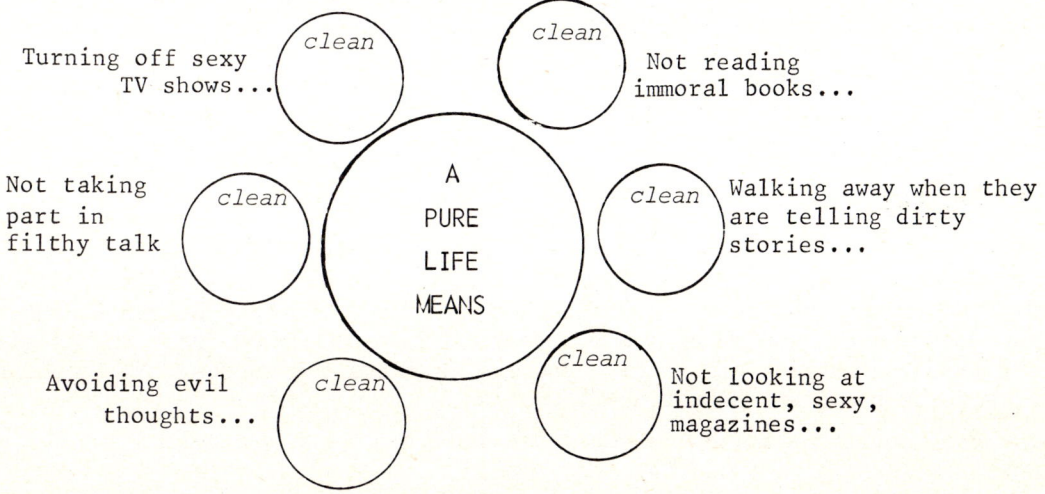

CHAPTER 11 — RESPONSIBLE CARETAKERS

God gives us our possessions and wants us to use them as his caretakers. He protects property by forbidding all forms of stealing. He wants us to be honest in all our dealings and to take good care of our own and our neighbours' property.

READ "GROWING..." pages 49-51.

THINK about:

1. What it means that we are God's stewards;
2. Ways in which you are dishonest;
3. How respect for our neighbours' property would show itself;

TIME FOR REFLECTION

What should these people do or say in the following situations as followers of Jesus? Find texts from page 51 which tell you, and write in the references.

a. Jacquie is having problems with a test. Suddenly she notices that she can read what her friend alongside is writing. ....

b. A collector for the Freedom from Hunger Campaign comes to the door of Mary's house and asks for money to help feed the starving. ....

c. Michael wants to sell his old car. Another man suggests that he patch up and paint over some bad rust spots and wind back the speedo to get a better price. ....

d. Sally offers to sell Ann a transistor radio for a very cheap price. Ann suspects that it is actually stolen goods. ....

e. Don is very small for his age so he often travels on the bus as a child, even though he is actually too old. ....

FOR DEVOTIONS

A A story is told about young Abraham Lincoln. At the time he was a grocer. Once when he accidentally charged a customer 6¢ too much he walked three miles after work to return the money. Another time he discovered that he had charged a customer for two ounces of goods more than he had weighed out. So, he closed his shop and hurried off to give the man an extra two ounces. No wonder he came to be known as "Honest Abe"!

"Honesty in little things is not a little thing!" Do you agree?
How does Lincoln show us what this means?

READ 1 Thessalonians 4:9-12. THINK about how we can show love for our neighbour by respecting his rights and property.

B READ Leviticus 19:35. REPEAT Ephesians 4:28

"To be honest in this world is to be one person picked out of ten thousand."
(Shakespeare)

Why did Shakespeare say this?
THINK about why it is so important for Christians to be honest.

C ASK God in prayer ... to forgive you your sins of dishonesty;
... to make you thankful for Jesus, your perfect Saviour;
... to help you take good care of your own and your neighbours' property.

FAMILY TIME

During family worship you could READ hymn 367 and then DISCUSS together what it means that we are God's stewards.
READ 1 Thessalonians 4:9-12 and talk about the style of life suggested by the text.
Close with the Lord's Prayer.

MORE TO DO

There are many forms of stealing.

Fill out the snake by completing the words:
STEALING:

... by using force - R . . . . . .

... by ruining public property - V . . . .

... by threatening to reveal someone's secret - B . . . .

... by breaking into someone's house - B . . . .

... by copying someone's signature - F . . . . . .

... by tricking people - F . . . .

... by making false money C . . . .

A loving, honest heart shows itself in various ways. Find five ways suggested on p. 50 of "Growing..."

A LOVING HONEST HEART

CHAPTER 12
SPEAKING IN LOVE

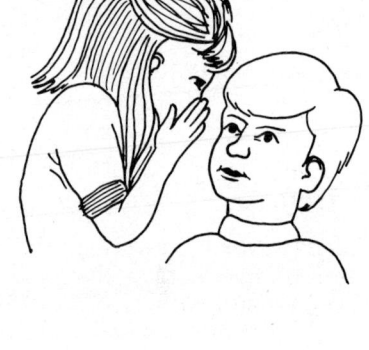

God commands us to speak the truth at all times. He forbids us to tell lies or to speak in any way that harms other people. We are to speak up for our neighbour and protect him from anything which might hurt his good name.

READ "GROWING..." pages 53-55.

THINK about what you have read by putting together these sentences in their proper order.

a. In the Eighth Commandment God protects... ... but also to betray him.

b. God forbids us not only to tell lies about our neighbour... ... to defend our neighbour and to speak well of him.

c. We can also harm our neighbour's good name... ... our own and our neighbour's good name.

d. God wants us to do all that we can... ... by spreading gossip about him.

TIME FOR REFLECTION

A shop near the school had been broken into and some money stolen. Everybody at school was talking about how it had happened and who might have done it.

"Do you know those people who came to live in our street?" Jerry asked his group. "You mean Bob's family?" Carl asked.

"Yes." replied Jerry. "Have you met his older brother, Stan? Well, someone told me that he had been in trouble with the police before he came to live here. Yesterday I saw him in the amusement parlour and he was sure spending a lot of money! Do you reckon it was him?"

"I know him," said Barry. "He seems a an odd kind of guy. I wouldn't be surprised if he did it."

"That's just not true," said Alex angrily. "I know Stan. He got into trouble for driving his car too fast, but he's an honest guy. He had a birthday the other day and I know he got some money. You'd better not start spreading rumours about him!"

a. Imagine you are Stan. *How would you feel about what Jerry said?*
   How would you feel about Alex?
b. Imagine you are Jerry. *How would you feel about what Alex said?*
   How would you feel if Stan heard what you said?
c. Think about this story and find an example of <u>betraying</u> another person, of <u>slandering</u>, of <u>defending</u> him, and of <u>explaining his actions</u> in a kind way.

FOR DEVOTIONS

A READ *Proverbs 11:9-13.* Note how the writer contrasts the harm done by evil speech with the blessings which come through wise and loving speech.
  APPLY these verses to your own life as you think about how you speak of others.

B Here is a good guide for you to follow when you start talking about others:

        Is what I am going to say true?
        Is it necessary? Is it loving?

REPEAT *the memory verses:* Matthew 7:1; James 4:11; 1 Peter 4:18.

How does this guide sum up the three texts?
How does it guide you in keeping the Eighth Commandment?

C Jesus followed this guide perfectly for us.
  God forgives us our many sins of the tongue because of Jesus.
  PRAY, asking God ... to forgive you for breaking the Eighth Commandment,
  ... to help you always to speak in love.

FAMILY TIME

READ *James 3:3-10* with your family and DISCUSS the guide for speaking about others.
TALK about how this guide could be helpful in family life.
READ *hymn 357, v. 3, as a prayer.*

MORE TO DO

Answer the questions to find the code. Use the code to decipher the text.

A	Whom we are not to speak against	A	$\overline{1}\,\overline{2}\,\overline{3}\,\overline{4}\,\overline{5}\,\overline{6}\,\overline{7}\,\overline{8}\,\overline{9}$
B	Telling lies about others	B	$\overline{1}\,\overline{2}\,\overline{3}\,\overline{4}\,\overline{5}\,\overline{6}\,\overline{7}$
C	Revealing secrets	C	$\overline{1}\,\overline{2}\,\overline{3}\,\overline{4}\,\overline{5}\,\overline{6}\,\overline{7}\,\overline{8}\,\overline{9}$
D	An untruth	D	$\overline{1}\,\overline{2}\,\overline{3}$
E	To speak up for others	E	$\overline{1}\,\overline{2}\,\overline{3}\,\overline{4}\,\overline{5}\,\overline{6}$
F	The opposite of 'speak well' of others	F	$\overline{1}\,\overline{2}\,\overline{3}\,\overline{4}\,\overline{5}\ \overline{6}\,\overline{7}\,\overline{8}\,\overline{9}$
G	The way we should explain our neighbours' actions	G	$\overline{1}\,\overline{2}\,\overline{3}\,\overline{4}\,\overline{5}\,\overline{6}$

"
B5 A7 E5 A7 C3 B1 F2 A2 C5 F5 C2 F7 D2 B2 F4 A4 B3 G2 G3 F1 C3 A7 B4 F6

F4 B4 A7 C3 A5 F3 C4 A6 B7 D3 C3 A5 C4 F6 B4."

13 WHAT DO YOU WANT?
CHAPTER

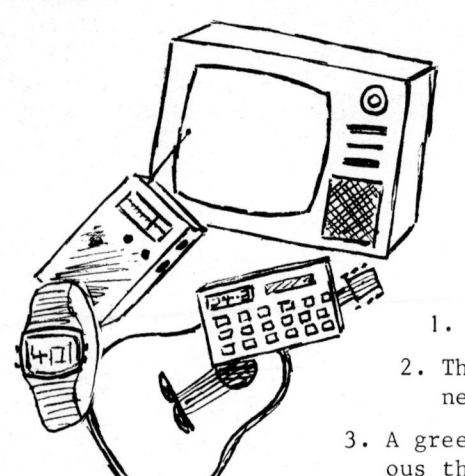

God demands that all our thoughts and desires should be holy. He forbids all coveting, all greed and jealousy which make us slaves of things and ruin our relationships with others. We are to be content with what we have and help our neighbour keep what belongs to him.

READ "GROWING..." pages 57-59.

CORRECT these sentences:

1. Our desire to get something is coveting.
2. The Tenth Commandment forbids us to covet our neighbours' property.
3. A greedy, jealous person is less likely to have covetous thoughts.
4. Advertising has such a big influence because most people are content with what they have.
5. God doesn't expect us to help our neighbour keep what is his if he has done us wrong.
6. Being content with what we have will not guard us against coveting if we are very poor.

TIME FOR REFLECTION

FIND the word below which best suits the attitude of these people.
TICK those people who are pleasing to God.

a. Ted was angry because he wasn't picked in the football team, so now he won't talk to some of the team. _____
b. Mary doesn't have fine clothes like some other girls because her family can't afford them, but she doesn't complain. _____
c. Frank stole a good biro and said he was given it for his birthday. _____
d. Sam told Caroline lies about her boyfriend because he wanted her to go with him. _____
e. Gwen saw a fine pair of jeans in the shop and started saving her money to buy them. _____
f. When John saw Jim with a new pocket calculator he started planning how he might steal it. _____
g. When June complained about some of the girls in her netball team and said she wouldn't play any more, Betty suggested that she talk it over with her coach. _____

coaxing away *scheming to get* *desiring in the right way*
being contented *encouraging loyalty* *being jealous*
pretending to have a right to it

FOR DEVOTIONS

A *THINK* about this quote from a modern author:

"Our society encourages us to think that the more we get the happier we'll be. Plenty of money, a fine home, motor cars, electrical goods, records and cassettes, good clothes - these are supposed to give us the good life and make us contented. But there's a terrible trap in all this! So often we discover that the more we get the more we want and we end up miserably discontented. Let's never forget that the most important things for a happy life are loving relationships with God and other people."

Do you agree?

READ *Proverbs 30:7-9.* *Why does the writer not want to be poor?*
Why doesn't he want to be rich?
What can you learn from these verses?

B SAY *the memory verse, 1 Timothy 6:8-10 and think about this story:*

A young man said he was going to get very rich. "The worst thing in life is to be poor," he told his friend. "You're wrong, Bill!" his friend replied. "The worst thing in life is to be without God."

What did Bill's friend mean?
READ *Philippians 4:11-13 and see whether Paul would agree with the friend.* Paul says he has learnt the secret of contentment. *What is the secret?* *(see verses 6 and 7)*

C READ *hymn 299, "My God accept my heart this day", as a prayer. Ask God to forgive you your sins of covetousness and to give you a holy heart.*

FAMILY TIME

READ *Proverbs 30:7-9* with your family and DISCUSS what it says. You could read the quote above or the story about Bill and talk about it. Use hymn 299 as a family prayer.

MORE TO DO

What are the five things you would like to have most? What will it cost you to get them? As you fill out the chart, think about this and decide if you still want them.

5 THINGS I WOULD MOST LIKE TO HAVE	TEMPTATIONS I MIGHT FACE IN GETTING THEM	DO I STILL WANT THEM?	HOW WILL I GET THEM?
1			
2			
3			
4			
5			

DRAW *your own dragon of lust:*

LOOK UP *Ephesians 6:17* and draw the weapon God gives you to destroy the dragon of lust:

14 CHAPTER
WHAT'S THE PENALTY?

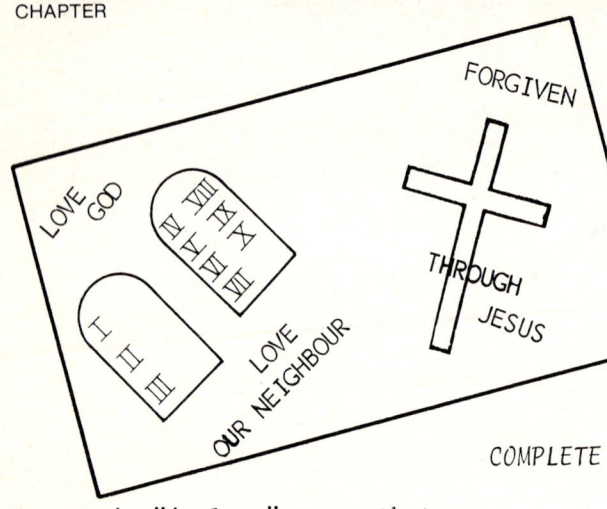

God demands that we keep his commandments perfectly, in thoughts, words, and deeds. Because of our sinfulness we continually break God's commandments and deserve his anger and punishment. Yet God is gracious to us for Jesus' sake and offers forgiveness in his name. As God's forgiven people we want to live according to his commandments and gladly to do his will.

READ "GROWING..." pages 61-63.

COMPLETE these sentences:

1. God is "jealous" means that

2. Original sin is

3. Actual sin is

4. The punishment for sin is

TIME FOR REFLECTION

THINK about these situations and write in your answers:

a. Some friends from the church were visiting Mr. Brown, talking to him about God and his need of Jesus. "Why all this talk about sin," he said. "Sure, I'm not perfect, but I live a good life, give money to charity and never do anyone any harm. Why should I be worried about God or a Saviour?"

What should the visitors say?

b. Neville got involved with a gang which stole second-hand cars and sold the parts. An old friend warned Neville about this. Later on Neville made fun of this friend and said, "Nobody's going to tell me what to do! I'll never get caught."

What would you say to Neville?

c. Mrs. Robertson told her husband that their new baby needed to be baptized. "Why?" asked Mr. Robertson, who was not a Christian. "So that Jesus might wash his sins away," she replied. "But our baby hasn't done anything wrong!" said Mr. Robertson.

What could she reply?

d. The chaplain of the jail was talking to a man found guilty of serious crimes. He spoke about the punishment for sin and how God wants to forgive us for Jesus' sake. "There's no hope for me," the prisoner said. "I can't be forgiven; I've done too many really bad things."

What should the chaplain say?

FOR DEVOTIONS

How do you feel about sin and God's Law? God tells us in his Word how we should feel. Look up the texts and decide which one matches best with the feelings:

1 John 1:8,9; Isaiah 1:18; Psalm 130:3,4; Romans 1:18.

When you forget that sin makes God angry. ....
When you feel scared of God because of your sin. ....
When you think you're pretty good and don't feel
a need for the Saviour. ....
When you feel doubtful if God could forgive you
because of some bad sin. ....

FAMILY TIME

Perhaps your family could join in making the poster on page 28. You could display this in your home.
You could read through the Ten Commandments with your family. Close with a prayer thanking God for Jesus, the Saviour, and asking him to help you live according to his will.

MORE TO DO

Review the Ten Commandments as you do this crossword:

CLUES:
Across:
2. Speaking evil of God.
3. What we are to do for our neighbour when his good name is attacked.
6. The number of commandments in the second table.
8. What God's representatives have over us.
9. What we are to do for our neighbour in his physical needs.
11. What God threatens to do to those who break his commandments.
13. The teaching of the Bible which tells us of Jesus our Saviour.
17. Worship of false gods.
18. What we are called as God's caretakers.
19. One reason why we should keep the commandments.
20. What we are to do with God's Word.
21. A sin forbidden by the Second Commandment.

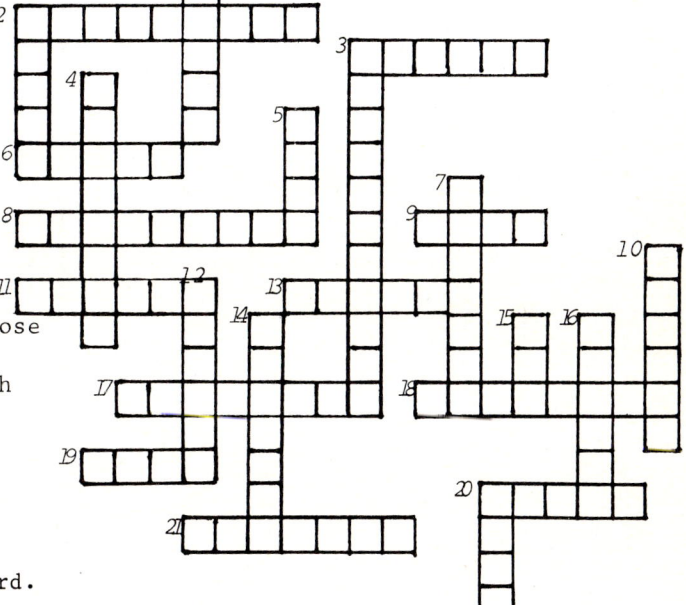

Down:
1. The number of commandments in the first table.
2. What God promises to do for those who keep his commandments.
3. How we are not to get our neighbour's property.
4. Sinful desire for anything.
5. The kind of heart God wants us to have.
7. What we are not to do with God's commandments.
10. The person through whom we have hope of forgiveness.
12. How we are to regard our parents.
14. Telling lies about our neighbour.
15. The teaching of the Bible which shows us God's anger over sin.
16. One way in which we may break the Fifth Commandment.
20. Another reason why we should keep the commandments.

CHAPTER 15

UNIT TWO: THE CREED
CONFESSING OUR CHRISTIAN FAITH

In the Creed, Christians confess their faith in God. Through his Word, God makes himself known to us as the Triune God, the Father, the Son, and the Holy Spirit. He is unlimited in his power, his holiness, and his love for us. Through faith we have a personal relationship with him and trust him as our Creator, our Saviour, and the One who makes us holy.

READ "GROWING..." pages 65-67.

THINK about these questions:

1. Why do Christians confess the Creed?
2. How has God made himself known to us?
3. What special work does God do for us as the Father? the Son? the Holy Spirit?
4. What does it mean that God is unlimited?

TIME FOR REFLECTION

In each of these stories a person has a wrong attitude to God.
WRITE in what this is and what you could say to help.

a. Peter and Tim were talking about the Christian faith. Tim did not believe in God. Peter confessed his faith and said, "I believe there is a God and I know that he cares for me". "How can you be so sure," Tim replied. "You've never seen him!"

b. A pastor was teaching a group of people about God. He explained how the true God is three Persons in one God. "That couldn't be right," said Mr. Ford. "You can't have it both ways. Either there are three different gods or there is just one God with three different names."

c. Sam's science class learnt about the greatness of the universe. "If the universe is that big," Sam told Julie later, "God couldn't be present everywhere."

d. Paul had done something very wrong. As he thought about what he had done he said to himself, "How could God love me? I'm too great a sinner!"

FOR DEVOTIONS

A St. Augustine was a famous Christian teacher from early times. One day he was walking along the sea-shore thinking about the mystery of the Holy Trinity. "How can there be three Persons equal in power and glory but only one God?" he was thinking. Just then he noticed a little girl playing in the sand. She had dug a hole in the sand and was running to and fro from the sea filling a sea-shell with water and pouring it into the hole. "What are you trying to do?" he asked. "I'm filling the sea into this hole," she replied.

Augustine smiled to himself. Fancy trying to fit the ocean into a little hole! And then he suddenly thought, "But that's what I've been doing! Trying to understand the Triune God with my little mind."

Why couldn't Augustine fit God into his brain?

READ Psalm 139:1-12 and think about how great God is.
How does his greatness make you feel? Why can you be glad to have such an almighty loving God?

B *READ Isaiah 6:1-4. How do the angels praise the Triune God?*

Christians still sing this hymn of praise. See how it is used in the liturgy of Holy Communion (Lutheran Hymnal p. 11).
Say these words as your own hymn of praise to the Triune God.

C REPEAT *the memory verse 2 Corinthians 13:14 and Numbers 6:24-26.*
THINK *about* how you have experienced God as Father, Son, and Holy Spirit.
Why is this teaching so important for your life as a Christian?

FAMILY TIME
You could ask members of the family to help make symbols of the Holy Trinity and display them in your home.
READ Psalm 139:1-12 and TALK about how God is described by the psalmwriter.
Close with the Lord's Prayer and the Benediction (Numbers 6:24-26).

MORE TO DO
Here are some symbols of the Holy Trinity. Write in what you think they teach about God.

Design your own symbol. You could use triangles, circles or flowers like the fleur-de-lis.

CHAPTER 16 — GOD HAS CREATED ME

 God the Father is the Creator of all things in heaven and earth. He made Adam and Eve in his image as the crown of all that he had made on earth. He is <u>our</u> Maker. All good things in life come from him. When we think of <u>his</u> great work of creation we want to serve and praise him as OUR God and Father.

READ "GROWING..." pages 69-71.

MARK these sentences true or false:

1. ...We can be sure that God is the Creator because science has proved it.
2. ...God created the earth out of material which has always existed.
3. ...The wonder and beauty of nature show us the greatness of the Creator.
4. ...Only the Father and not the Son and the Holy Spirit took part in creation.
5. ...God is not <u>my</u> Maker because I received life through my parents.
6. ...The real parents of the human race are primates, not Adam and Eve.
7. ...God did not create the devil because he couldn't make anything evil.
8. ...I can praise the Creator by serving and obeying him all my life.

TIME FOR REFLECTION

A group of young people went to a camp in the mountains for a long weekend. It was beautiful country - forests, mountains, valleys, and a stream rushing down to a lake.

On the Saturday afternoon they all went for a hike down to the lake and back. That evening they had good fun and fellowship at a social and an impromptu concert. Later that night, they sat around a campfire under the trees. The whole group was rather silent as they drank in the beauty of the moonlit scene.

The leader led them in a devotion. He asked members of the group to share an experience they had enjoyed that day. "It's great to get out into the country," said Bob. "We had a good time on the hike," said Cheryl, "and all those beaut views were fantastic!" "I didn't know so many kids could do all those things," said Jenny, referring to the impromptu concert.

The leader summed up the day for all of them when he thanked God for the beauty of nature and for the good gifts he had given them. They all enjoyed singing songs which praised God the Creator.

When have you felt like the group gathered around the campfire?

Write down times you have especially appreciated the beauty of nature	Write down some talents which God has given you

FOR DEVOTIONS

A "Whoever looks on this universe without admiring the wonder of all that God has made and without praising him for his creation, is like a pair of glasses without eyes to see through them." *(Carlyle)*

What does Carlyle mean? *(Romans 1:19,20 will help you answer.)*

READ *Psalm 33:1-9.* Why does the believer want to praise God when he considers all the wonders of nature?
How can you serve your heavenly Father?

B READ *Psalm 139:13-18.* As you read the psalm, THINK *about* the wonder of your body and the life which God has given you.

In prayer ... thank God for all the good things he has given you;
... ask him to help you to use your life for his praise and the welfare of other people.

C REPEAT *the memory verse Genesis 1:27 and* THINK about what it means for you as a Christian that God made Adam and Eve in his image.

FAMILY TIME

Are there any pictures or paintings of scenes of nature in your home. If there are, the family could TALK about them, saying why they like them. You could READ *Psalm 33:1-9* and the family could share experiences of how they appreciate nature. FIND a Christian poem or song which tells of the beauty of creation and use this for the devotion. (For example, How Great Thou Art.)

MORE TO DO

This is a scene from nature. Complete it by drawing in the items missing. The numbers are the verses of Psalm 104 which tell you what to draw.

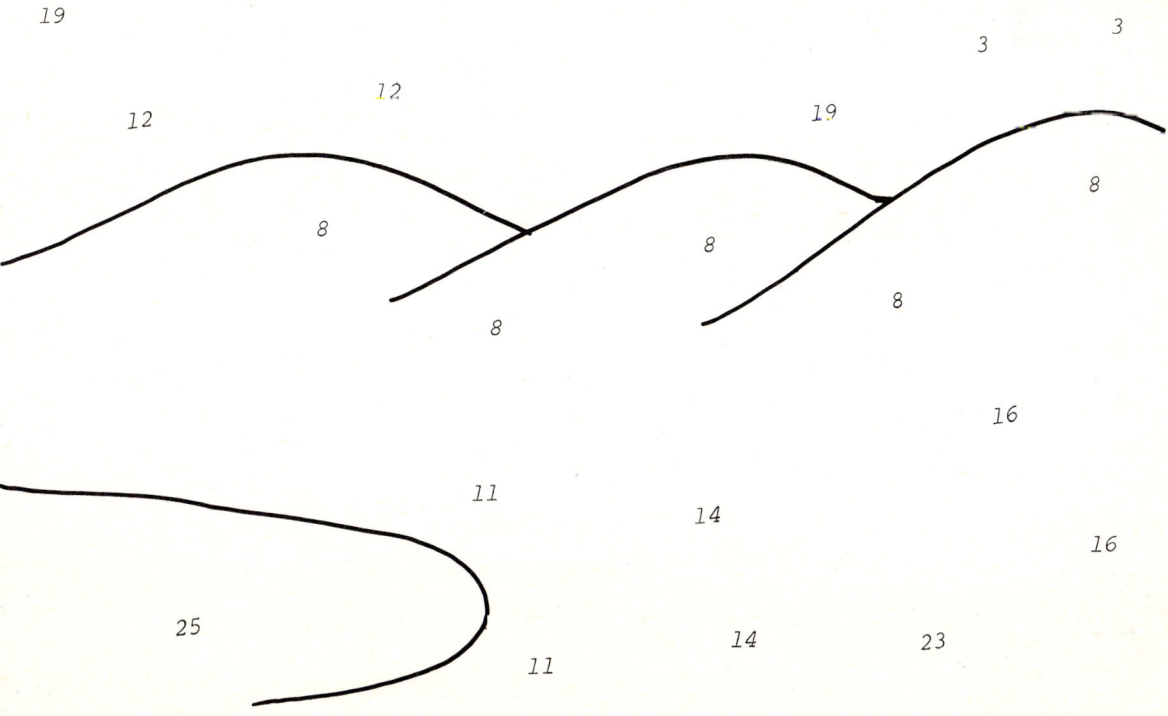

CHAPTER 17 — GOD CARES FOR US

God cares for all that he has made. We are completely dependent on our heavenly Father. Although we don't deserve it, he provides us with all that we need for life on earth. He protects us from danger and helps us in trouble. We can show our love and trust in him by being thankful and living for his glory.

READ "GROWING..." pages 73-75.

COMPLETE these sentences:

God preserves us out of his .... and ..... even though we are .... He .... for us in many ways. Through the .... of ...... he gives us our .... . He uses many ...... to .... for us and provide for us. Because of ... the world is full of .... and we face many .... Yet God .... to be with us to .... us. We can show our .... by praising and .... him all our .... .

(help   thankfulness   mercy   laws   people   nature   sin   promises   food   dangers   life   goodness   troubles   serving   care   sinners   provides)

TIME FOR REFLECTION

The people in these stories show that they trust in God to care for them. Find a text from "Growing..." pages 73-75 which suits and write in the reference.

a. Stan was very sick. As he lay in hospital he often felt downhearted. Then he would cheer up when he thought of how God loved him. "I don't really have to worry," he thought. "God is taking care of me even though I'm sick."

b. Mr. Heinrich was very thankful for his good harvest. He made a generous offering at the Thanksgiving Service. "God is very good to me," he told the pastor. "I don't really deserve all he has given me."

c. Sally was reading a book about animals. The book showed how animal life was adapted to different parts of the earth, such as deserts, rain forests, the polar regions. "Isn't it wonderful how God feeds the animals wherever they live," she said to her sister.

d. Mr. Evans was taking his family for an outing. Their car collided with another car at an intersection. The car was badly damaged, but none of the family were seriously hurt.
"We can thank God that we weren't seriously injured," Mr. Evans said to his wife and children.

FOR DEVOTIONS

A A ferry ran into a bad storm crossing the bay. Some of the passengers were really scared. But one little boy seemed quite unafraid. A woman noticed how he kept on cheerfully playing with his toys and asked him whether he wasn't afraid. "Why should I be scared?" he replied. "My dad's the captain of this boat!"

Christians feel like that about their whole life. Why?

READ Psalm 121. THINK about different ways in which God has cared for you during the past week. Thank him for this.

B Felix of Nola was a Christian saint from early times. Once, when persecution broke out he had to flee from his enemies who wanted to kill him. As he fled, he crawled into a cave to escape. As he lay in the darkness spiders wove their webs across the narrow entrance. When his enemies rode up they noticed the webs and went on, thinking he couldn't be in there. Felix was very thankful. He said, "When God isn't there a wall is only like a spider's web. When God is there a spider's web is like a wall!"

What did he mean? When we have troubles and feel worried, what should we do?

READ Philippians 4:4-7. Tell God right now about all your worries and ask him to give you his peace.

C WRITE a responsive prayer praising God. You could begin like this:

    For all you have done for me today, *I praise you, heavenly Father...*

FAMILY TIME

TALK to your parents about times when your family has been saved from danger or accident.
READ Psalm 121 together.
Use your responsive prayer to close the devotion.

MORE TO DO

God has an important message for you. Read what is says by using the morse code. (Symbols are on page 11.)

.- .-.. .-- .- -.-- ...   .- .-. .   .-- .- - -.-. .... .. -. --.

.-- --- .-. .-. .. . .- -. -..   .-- .. - .... --

-... . - .-. .- -.-- . -..   .... .   -.-. .- .-. . ...

..-. --- .-.   -.-- --- ..-

CHAPTER 18: JESUS OF NAZARETH

Christians joyfully confess that Jesus Christ is the Son of God who came to earth to save us. He was born of the Virgin Mary and lived as the Saviour in Palestine almost 2000 years ago. By living, dying and rising again for us, Jesus has saved us from sin and given us the hope of eternal life.

READ "GROWING..." pages 77-79.

How well do you know the story of Jesus? NUMBER these sentences in their right order so that they tell the story of Jesus.

... The Jewish leaders began to hate Jesus and plotted to kill him.
... When Jesus was 30 years old he was baptized by John.
... Three days later he rose from the dead.
... Jesus was born in Bethlehem when Herod was king.
... For about 3 years Jesus travelled around Palestine, teaching and helping people in trouble.
... Pontius Pilate had Jesus crucified outside Jerusalem.
... After 40 days he ascended into heaven.
... Jesus grew up in Nazareth in Galilee.
... When Judas betrayed him, Jesus was led away for trial.

TIME FOR REFLECTION

WRITE down the attitude these people are showing. THINK about why these are good attitudes.

a. James was confused when some boys told him the Christmas story was just a fairy story. That evening he read the Gospel stories about Jesus' birth and asked God to give him a firm faith.

b. Bob's cousin never went to church and didn't seem to know anything about Jesus. One day Bob spoke to him about Jesus, telling him how much the Saviour meant to him. "It's great to know that Jesus is our friend," he said.

c. John's friend asked him some questions about Jesus' life. John found that he couldn't answer him very well, so he started to read through the Gospel of Matthew.

d. Mr. Jones and his friends were having a discussion about the end of the world. Mr. Jones told them he was sure that Jesus would return one day to judge. "You can be quite sure about that," Mr. Jones said. "Jesus told us himself."

FOR DEVOTIONS

A Cecil Rhodes was a famous man who helped build the British Empire in Africa. As he lay dying, he is reported to have said, "So much to do! So little done!" When Jesus was dying on the cross he called out, "It is finished!" All the work God had given him to do he had done - perfectly.

THINK about what this means for you: Jesus has done all that is needed for you to be saved. He is your perfect Saviour.

READ Hebrews 2:14-18. Why did Jesus become a true human being? (14)
What did he do as our high priest? (17)
What does it mean for you that Jesus suffered and was tempted? (18)

B *READ Acts 13:22-33 for a summary of Jesus' life.*

Which events does St. Paul speak about? (See vss. 23, 29, 30)
Why does he focus on these events?

...Thank God for sending his Son to be your Saviour.
...Tell Jesus that you want him to be your Lord.
...Ask him to be with you day by day to help you live as his disciple.

C *REPEAT the memory verse Philippians 2:7,8.* THINK *about* what it means that Jesus took the form of a servant, and what it cost him to finish the work God had given him.
Why did Jesus do all this?

FAMILY TIME

You could *READ* pages 78, 79 from "Growing..." as a devotion with your family and *TALK about* the illustrations. *READ* or sing the hymn, "Once in Royal David's City" (Lutheran Hymnal 632) for your devotion.

MORE TO DO

FILL OUT the map. What important events happened at these places? Look up the Scripture references to find out. Fill out the acrostic and write in the places on the map.

1. Matthew 3:5,6   J _ _ _ _ _
2. Matthew 2:5   _ E _ _ _ _ _ _ _
3. Matthew 15:21   S _ _ _ _
4. Luke 13:33   _ _ _ U _ _ _ _
5. Matthew 16:13   _ _ _ S _ _ _ _
6. Matthew 8:5, 14   C _ _ _ _ _ _ _ _
7. John 12:1   _ _ _ H _ _ _
8. Luke 19:1   _ _ R _ _ _ _
9. Matthew 4:23   _ _ _ I _ _ _
10. John 4:5   S _ _ _ _ _
11. Matthew 2:23   _ _ _ _ _ _ T _

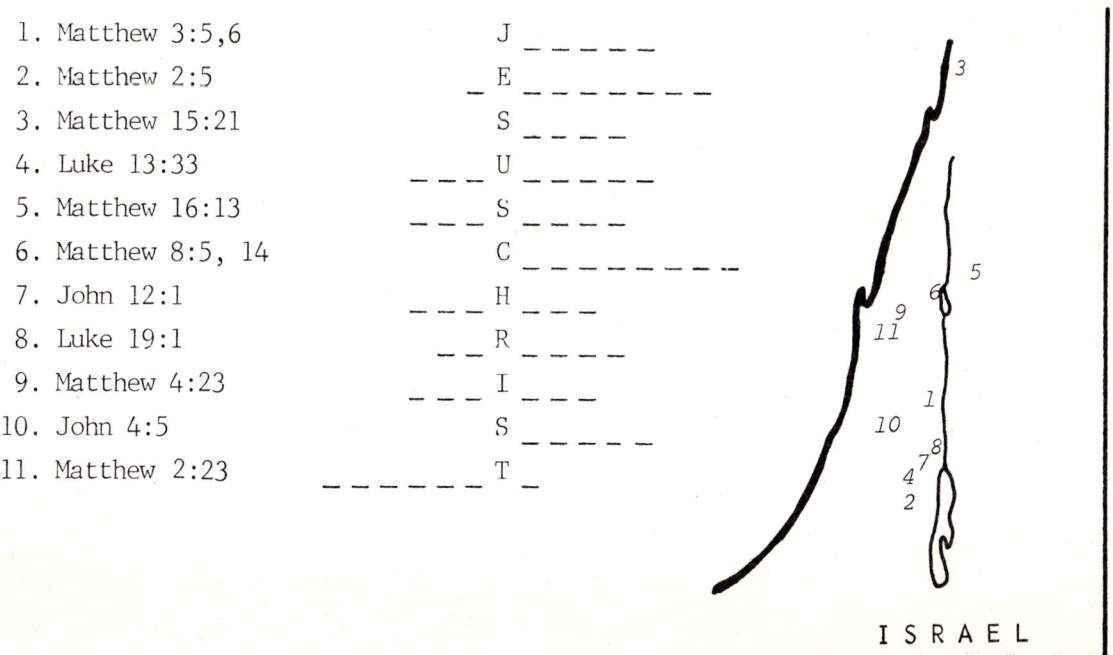

ISRAEL

CHAPTER 19 — GOD WITH US

Jesus is true God and true man. The eternal Son of God became man, born of the Virgin Mary. It was necessary for our Saviour to be God and man in order to save us. Each Christian makes his personal confession, "Jesus is my Lord!"

READ "GROWING..." pages 81-83.

THINK about the following questions:

1. Why can you be sure that Jesus is true God?
2. Why can you be sure that Jesus is true man?
3. Why did our Saviour need to be both God and man?

TIME FOR REFLECTION

WRITE down what you would say in reply to these statements. Find a text or a sentence from "Growing..." pages 81-83 which can help you.

a. "How can you be sure Jesus is God? He was born the same as we are."

b. "Aren't we supposed to worship only God? Then you shouldn't worship Jesus!"

c. "If Jesus is true God and also true man, he must be two persons."

d. "Why did God come himself to save us? Why didn't he just send a holy angel?"

e. "Suppose Jesus did live here on earth once. How does that affect me?"

f. "You say that Jesus is true God! Then surely he couldn't die on a cross."

FOR DEVOTIONS

A In a palace in Rome there is a ceiling with a fine painting of God in his heavenly glory. But the room is very small and the ceiling very high, so that it is hard to look up and see it properly. So the owner has placed a mirror on the floor so that people don't need to look up to see the painting of God in his glory. They only need to look down into the mirror.

In the same way, we can't see God by looking up. That is why Jesus came to make him known to us. Jesus reflects the glory of God so that through him we can really know God and be his friend.

READ John 1:14-18.   THINK about:
  ... how Jesus has made God known to YOU,
  ... how Jesus did not come to frighten you with God's power and majesty, but to show you the glory of God's love for you.

How do you feel about God when you think of all that Jesus has done for you?

B A young missionary in Africa adopted the native dress of the tribe with whom he was working. He wanted to be one with the people as he told them about Jesus. He sent a photo of himself back home. When his sister saw it she was shocked. "I can't believe that's really my brother," she said. "He's become an African!" "Yes," replied her pastor. "He has tried to become an African so that they might become Christians - and be saved."

READ Luke 5:27-32 and THINK about why Jesus is the friend of sinners.

Why does this story of Jesus make you sure that God is your friend?

C READ *the hymn* "Fairest Lord Jesus" (Lutheran Hymnal 152), as a prayer of praise to Jesus your Lord.

WRITE the following heading on a separate sheet of paper, and then fill out what you want to do for Jesus.

```
                    BECAUSE JESUS IS MY LORD I WILL -
   In my family life            At school              In my social life
```

FAMILY TIME

Members of the family may like to help you draw symbols of Jesus' name.
READ John 1:14-18 and then the story about the mirror reflecting the painting.
TALK *about* how Jesus reflects God for us.
You could close the devotion by reading or singing the hymn "Fairest Lord Jesus".

MORE TO DO

Look up the Scripture references listed below and then write in how the story shows you that Jesus is true God and true man.

	JESUS	
	True God	True Man
Matthew 14:22-27		
Mark 5:35-43		
Matthew 3:16 - 4:2		
Matthew 28:18-20		

CHAPTER 20 — JESUS IS MY SAVIOUR

By nature we are all lost in sin and need salvation. Jesus is the only Saviour from sin, death and the power of the devil. He redeemed us (set us free) by giving his holy life as a sacrifice for the sins of the world. We receive the blessings of forgiveness and salvation by faith when we trust in Jesus as our Redeemer.

READ "GROWING..." pages 85-87.

MATCH the statements with the best ending:

1. Jesus is the only Saviour
2. Jesus kept the Ten Commandments for us
3. Jesus has set us free from sin
4. Jesus redeemed us from death
5. Jesus has conquered Satan
6. Jesus died for the sins of all people.

... by dying for us and rising again from the dead.
... but we receive the blessing of forgiveness only through faith.
... by overcoming all his temptations.
... by bearing our guilt and punishment.
... because we sin against them all the time.
... because no-one else has overcome sin and death for us.

TIME FOR REFLECTION

TICK the ending which describes the better way for these people to feel:

a. When the criminal heard that Jesus died for the sins of the world:
   ... *he doubted whether this could include a criminal.*
   ... *he felt sure that he could be saved.*

b. When Mary did something very wrong:
   ... *she asked Jesus to forgive her and felt at peace with God.*
   ... *she felt too ashamed to own up to God.*

c. When Stan heard that Jesus died for him:
   ... *he felt it was wrong that Jesus should die in his place.*
   ... *he was thankful that Jesus had saved him.*

d. When Jill kept falling into sin:
   ... *she felt sure that Jesus would always forgive her and help her fight sin.*
   ... *she felt she could never be free from the power of sin.*

e. When Peter heard about Jesus dying on the cross:
   ... *he felt it wasn't very important for him because he didn't do many wrong things.*
   ... *he felt sorry that he had helped cause the Saviour so much suffering.*

FOR DEVOTIONS

A THINK *about* this modern parable:

A man fell into a muddy pit and broke his leg. He couldn't get himself out. Someone passed by and saw the troube he was in. "Poor fellow," he said. "What bad luck to fall in there! If you ever get out make sure you don't fall in again!" Then he walked on. Another person passed by and felt sorry for the man in the pit. "I feel really sorry for you and would like to help you. But I've got my best clothes on. Do you think you could scramble up halfway? Then I could help you up the rest of the way." But the man in the pit could hardly move. Sadly he watched the second man go away. Then another man came past.

He carried deep scars from bad injuries. Hearing the man's groans he had pity on him. Climbing down into the mud he picked up the man and climbed out of the pit with him.

REPEAT the memory verses Isaiah 53:5 and Acts 4:12 and THINK about what this parable tells you about how you have been saved.
WRITE a prayer or song of thanks to Jesus for his work as your Saviour.

B Here is another story to think about:

At a slave market a man paid a lot of money to buy a negro. The slave, in his hatred, decided to kill the man who had bought him. But the man turned to him kindly and said, "You are free! I bought you so that you could be free." The slave was so overcome with thankfulness that he threw away his knife and said, "I will gladly follow you and serve you for life!"

What does this story teach us about our life as a follower of Jesus?

READ 2 Corinthians 5:15. How can you show Jesus that you are living for him?

C In the hymn "When I survey the wondrous cross" (Lutheran Hymnal 54), Isaac Watts tells us how he treasures Jesus and his cross more than anything else.

READ Philippians 3:8-11 and see how St. Paul feels the same way. Use the hymn as your own prayer of dedication to Jesus.

FAMILY TIME

You could READ Isaiah 53:3-7 and then the story of the man in the pit. Let the family TALK about what this parable means. (Instead of this you could read p. 86 from "Growing...".) Use the hymn "When I survey the wondrous cross" as a closing prayer.

MORE TO DO

We can only get to heaven through Jesus. He is the way.
Unscramble his names and use them as bridges etc.

SSUJE   VISAROU   TSHRIC   REEEEDRM   KGNI   GHHI-ESIRTP   DOGO-DPHHSERE

CHAPTER 21 — CHRIST OUR VICTORIOUS LORD

By rising again from the dead Jesus showed that he had won a great victory over sin, death and the devil. After 40 days he ascended into heaven as the King of Kings. He will come again at the last day to judge all people. Christians joyfully celebrate Jesus' great victory. We share in this victory. We are glad to follow Jesus our Lord, live in his kingdom, and serve and worship him forever.

READ "GROWING..." pages 89-91.

If the following statements are true, circle the first letter; if false, the second letter.

- J H   Jesus' resurrection shows us that he is truly the Son of God.
- B E   Jesus showed himself alive to all the people in the city of Jerusalem.
- S T   Because Jesus lives we can be sure that our sins are forgiven.
- U X   We can be sure that we shall rise from the dead because Jesus rose.
- D S   Jesus descended into hell to suffer.

- L P   Jesus' ascension means that he entered his full glory as King.
- I W   Jesus is present everywhere ruling with almighty power.
- G V   Jesus' ascension means that he is no longer present with us in our lives.
- K E   Unbelievers expect Jesus to return to judge them.
- S L   Jesus will return to take his followers into eternal life.

TIME FOR REFLECTION

How do these people feel about Jesus' victory over sin and death?
WRITE in how you think they ought to feel and why.

a. The Osborne family felt sad because granny had died. The pastor comforted the family by telling them that the old lady died as a Christian and was safe with Jesus. At the burial service Mrs. Osborne burst into tears and told her husband, "We have lost Mum. Maybe I'll never see her again".

b. Little Anne was scared to go out in the dark. "You don't need to be afraid, Jesus is with you," her older sister told her. "I wouldn't bet on that," said her older brother. "I've certainly never seen him!"

c. The Green family went out in a boat fishing. A strong wind came up and the boat overturned, but all the family were rescued by another boat nearby. Later, Ruth was talking to her friend about it. "We could easily have drowned," she said. "Jesus was really looking after us!" "What's Jesus got to do with it?" the other girl asked. "I'd say it was good luck that a boat was close."

d. A man was walking around with a placard on his back saying, "REPENT SINNERS. JESUS IS COMING TO JUDGE". George laughed when he saw it. "What a crank," he said. "There'll never be a judgment day."

FOR DEVOTIONS

A Martin Luther faced many troubles and problems in the work of the Reformation. Sometimes he got sad and downhearted. Once his wife noticed how sad he was. She dressed herself in black – the usual sign of mourning for the dead – and went on quietly doing her work around the house. When Luther noticed that she was dressed in black he asked, "Katy, who has died that you should dress in black?" "Why, I thought Jesus must be dead," she replied. "You're so worried. But if Jesus is alive, then surely all will be well."

What might Luther have replied to Katy?

READ 2 Corinthians 4:13-18. What gave Paul courage to carry on his work despite great trouble? Why can we feel like Paul as we face life and its problems?

B When the King of England heard for the first time the beautiful 'Hallelujah Chorus' from Handel's 'Messiah', he was so moved that he stood up in honour of Christ. Since then it has been customary for the whole audience to rise for the singing of this chorus. The words are based on the song of the saints in heaven.

READ Revelation 5:9-14 and join with the angels in heaven in praise of Christ.

C REPEAT the meaning of the Second Article putting your own name in place of "I, me, my". WRITE a short prayer, thanking God for making you sure that Jesus has done his work for YOU.

FAMILY TIME

GATHER things you can use as symbols of Jesus' resurrection, such as a flower and bulb, an egg, a butterfly. READ 1 Corinthians 15:3-8 and have the family TALK about the Easter symbols. Close with your prayer of thanks for Jesus.

MORE TO DO

The steps below represent some of the facts about Jesus' life. Unscramble these events and write them in on the right step. Draw in the proper symbol to match each step.

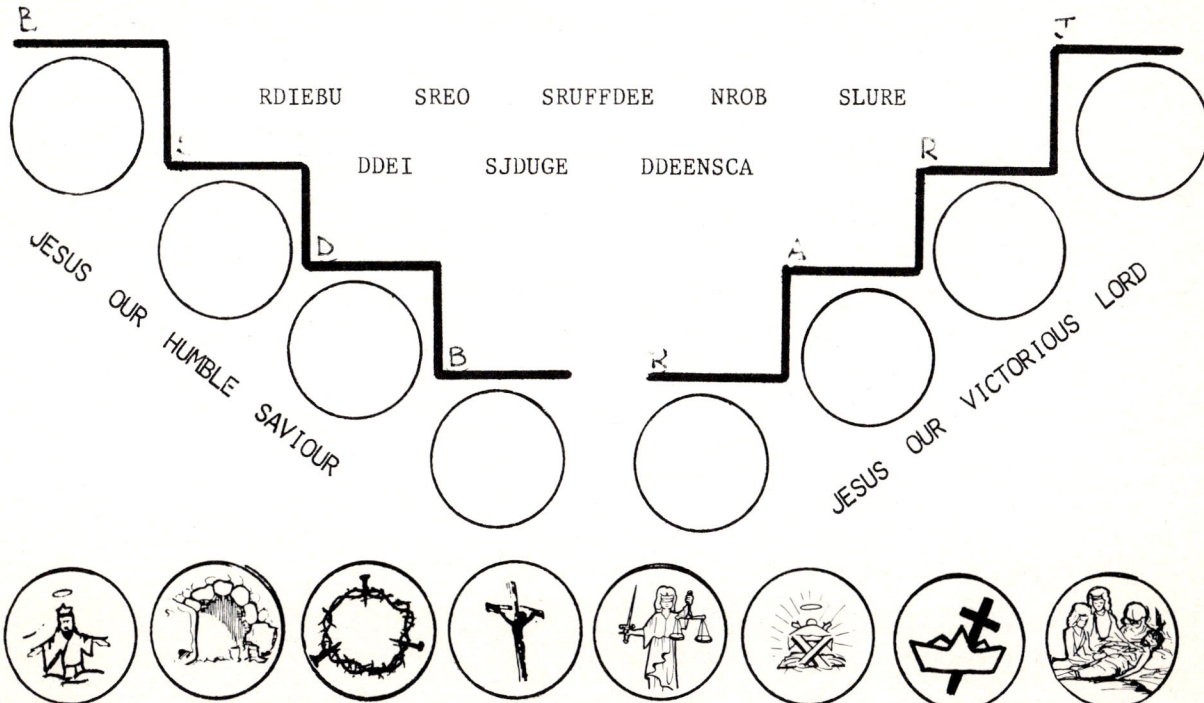

RDIEBU   SREO   SRUFFDEE   NROB   SLURE

DDEI   SJDUGE   DDEENSCA

JESUS OUR HUMBLE SAVIOUR

JESUS OUR VICTORIOUS LORD

CHAPTER 22

THE POWERFUL SPIRIT

The Holy Spirit is true God, the third person in the Holy Trinity. Because of our natural sinfulness, we can't make ourselves believers or live holy lives. The Holy Spirit worked through God's Word to convert us. He gave us faith in Christ so that we were born again as the children of God. He keeps us in the Christian faith and helps us grow in understanding God's Word and in living as the people of God.

READ "GROWING..." pages 93-95.

THINK about what you have read and complete these sentences:

1. The Holy Spirit is

2. We couldn't make ourselves Christians because we are

3. Sanctification means

4. The Holy Spirit called us through

5. In our daily lives the Holy Spirit

6. A good work in the sight of God is

TIME FOR REFLECTION

WRITE in whether these people are spiritually blind, dead, or enemies of God.

a. Wendy isn't interested in the church or in attending the services. "Why should I bother about worshipping God?" she asked. "I'm out to have a good time."

b. The communist guerillas told the people of a village that they would kill them and burn their houses if they kept on going to the Christian church services.

c. Brenton heard the pastor teaching how God forgives us because of Jesus. "What a load of rubbish," he said. "How can what someone did 2000 years ago help us today?"

How is the Holy Spirit helping these people?

a. Andy told his pastor he was glad that he understood the teachings of the Bible better because of confirmation lessons.

b. On his 90th birthday, Mr. Granger told his friends how thankful he was that God had looked after him all his life.

c. Bill felt depressed when he kept on doing the wrong thing, but he cheered up when he read the story of Jesus and Zacchaeus for devotion that evening.

FOR DEVOTIONS

A Here is a news item from a daily paper:

"BRAVE RESCUE FROM BURNING HOUSE - Two small children were rescued from a burning house in X St. last night. Firemen who rushed to the scene found a building well alight and a woman screaming that her two little children were inside. A fireman went inside through the smoke, past some rooms on fire, and managed to carry the children out to safety. Authorities commended the fireman for his great bravery."

THINK about how the Holy Spirit is our Rescuer and our Guide to safety.

READ 1 Corinthians 6:9-11 and see what the apostle says about the rescue operation of the Spirit.

B Have you ever seen the novelty known as "Magic Flowers"? What look like small dry pieces of wood or straw spread and grow into pretty flowers and leaves when put into a bowl of water. They seem quite dry and dead at first, then, in the water, as if by a miracle, they expand and blossom into flowers. The work of the Holy Spirit in our lives is rather like that. Under his influence our dry, dead hearts come alive for God as the Spirit leads us to love and trust God and fills our lives with the beauty of good works.

READ 1 Thessalonians 5:16-24 and THINK about the good works which you can do for God.

C READ Romans 15:13. WRITE a prayer thanking and praising the Holy Spirit for his work in you.

FAMILY TIME

Try to arrange a candle-light devotion with your family. GATHER around the light of the candle. SHOW your family the symbols of the Holy Spirit on pages 94 and 95 of "Growing..." and TALK about them. Then READ Acts 2:1-4. Close with hymn 131 from the Lutheran Hymnal.

MORE TO DO

Think about the Holy Spirit and his work as you fill out the crossword.

CLUES:
Across:
3. What the Spirit does when he shows us our need of a Saviour.
4. How we are by nature.
6. What the Spirit gives us.
9. What the Holy Spirit leads us to do in our lives.
10. The Third Person in the Trinity.

Down:
1. Being born again as a child of God.
2. The Spirit's work of making us holy.
5. The work of the Spirit in turning us around.
7. The means the Spirit uses to call us.
8. The relationship we have with God by nature.

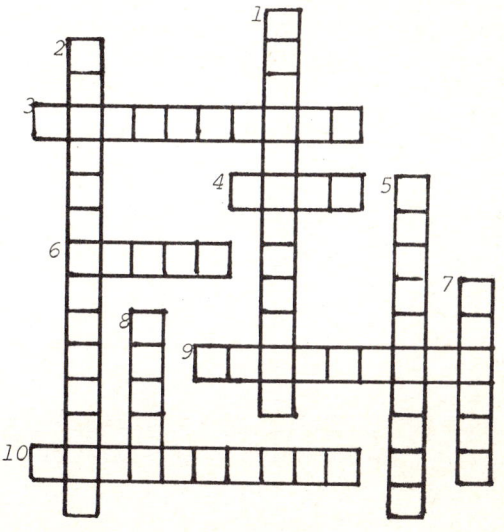

45

CHAPTER 23 — THE MEANS OF GRACE

The Word of God and the two Sacraments are the special means the Holy Spirit uses to make and keep us Christians. Through these means he brings us God's grace so that we receive forgiveness of sins and eternal life, and are given power to keep on growing as people of God. God wants us to be faithful in using the means of grace.

READ "GROWING..." pages 97-99.

CORRECT these sentences:

1. There are other means of grace besides the Word and the Sacraments.
2. Through the Law the Holy Spirit shows us that Jesus has saved us from sin.
3. Christ's command is not necessary for a sacrament.
4. The Holy Spirit can make us grow as Christians without the means of grace.
5. To repent means only to be sorry for your sins.
6. God does not use ordinary things like water, bread and wine to bring us his grace.

TIME FOR REFLECTION

FIND texts from pages 97-99 of "Growing..." which apply to these people. As you do this think about how you could show the same kind of attitudes.

a. Even though the boys at school laughed at Tom for being a Christian, he was glad he was a Christian and kept on trying to live for Christ.

b. Gwen had many doubts about God and Jesus, but when she heard the preacher at an evangelism service she became sure Jesus was her Saviour.

c. After she was confirmed Brenda kept on reading her Bible and liked to share in the Bible study at youth fellowship meetings.

d. The Smith family went to church regularly and enjoyed the meetings for Christian fellowship arranged by their congregation.

FOR DEVOTIONS

A Much of the country through which the River Murray runs is very dry. You drive through mile after mile of barren looking country. But what an amazing change occurs when you enter an irrigation area. Now all around you are green paddocks, orchards, vineyards, producing fruit and farm produce. This shows very clearly the power of water to change dry, barren country into fertile farms.

Why is this a good parable of the work of the Holy Spirit in our lives?

THINK about what these things represent in your life: dry, barren country; water which brings life and growth; good fruit and produce.

READ 1 Peter 1:22 - 2:2. THINK about how the Holy Spirit uses the Word of God as a power in your life.

B In 1812 the French army, under their famous leader Napoleon, retreated from Moscow in Russia. They faced a terrible winter. Hundreds froze to death. At night they would gather as closely as they could around fires to keep warm. But by morning many of the men furthest away from the fires had slowly frozen to death. They were too far away from the warmth of the fire.

READ verse 2 of the hymn 125 (Lutheran Hymnal) and THINK about how you as a Christian need the warmth which the Spirit gives through the Word of God.

C READ Luke 24:44-49 and THINK about what it means to be a witness for Jesus. If you have a friend who is not a Christian plan what you could say and do to help him come to know Jesus.

FAMILY TIME

You could READ "Grace to Grow" and "Use the Means of Grace" from page 99 of "Growing..." as a family devotion. Follow this by READING 1 Peter 1:22 - 2:2 and use hymn 125 as a prayer.

MORE TO DO

The Holy Spirit is like a stream of life-giving water as he works in our lives through the means of grace. Unscramble the words and write them in the proper places to see what this picture is teaching.

1. YHOL TIISPR   2. RCGAE   3. WORPE   4. DRWO FO DGO   5. SMTPABI
   6. SLRDO PPSURE   7. DOGO RKWSO   8. VOEL
         9. VICERES

CHAPTER 24 — GATHERED TOGETHER BY THE SPIRIT

The Holy Spirit gathers all believers in Christ into the holy Christian Church. This is the family of God. There is only one holy Church and Christ is its head. We believe in this Church because we can't tell exactly who belongs to it. But wherever the means of grace are used and Christian congregations gather for worship, there are members in this family of God.

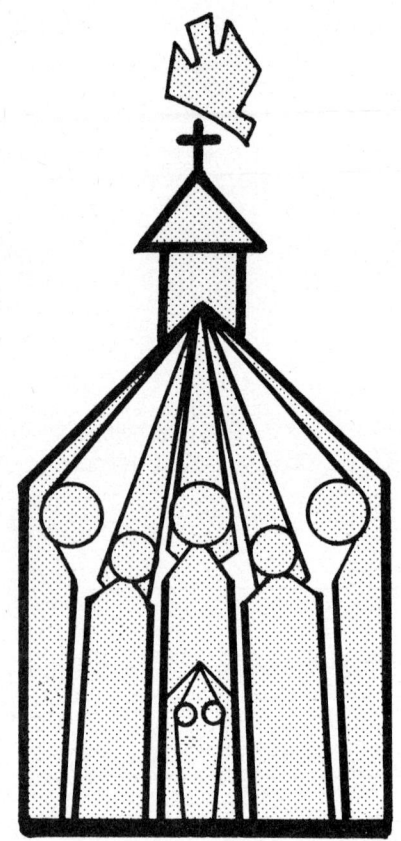

READ "GROWING..." pages 101-103.

CIRCLE any of the endings which are correct:

1. The Holy Spirit gathers people into the holy Christian Church:
   a. from all over the world;
   b. mainly from the rich and well educated;
   c. whatever the colour of their skin.

2. People become members of the holy Christian Church:
   a. because some are better than others;
   b. through the means of grace;
   c. when the Spirit gives them faith in Jesus.

3. The one holy Christian Church is:
   a. the communion of saints;
   b. all believers, united as God's people;
   c. divided up into many denominations.

4. The Church is holy because:
   a. its members are forgiven their sins;
   b. the Holy Spirit leads its members to live holy lives;
   c. people make themselves holy to join.

5. The Christian congregation:
   a. is the same as the holy Christian Church;
   b. may include hypocrites;
   c. is a group of Christians gathered together in one place to worship and serve God.

TIME FOR REFLECTION

"Are you going to church this morning," Sheryl asked her brother Ken. "Uh huh," he mumbled, still half asleep. "Well, you'd better hurry up and get ready. We'll be leaving soon." The family was ready at last and they drove off. They had about 5 km to travel. "I hope we won't be late," said Mum, who was usually worried about them not being on time. "Oh, now we have the new church," Ken replied, "there's always plenty of room." Sheryl liked their new church. It had some beautiful stained-glass windows. One window pictured Jesus and the apostles. Another showed him with the saints in heaven. These windows made Sheryl think about all the people who had believed in Jesus down through the centuries. She knew that one day she would actually see Jesus in his glory with all other believers. Finally they arrived and parked near the big new sign: "ST. PAUL'S LUTHERAN CHURCH, KINGSWOOD". They had a visiting preacher that day, who preached a mission sermon. After the service he spoke about the work their church was doing at home and overseas. As they drove back from church, Sheryl decided that one day she would like to work for the church as a parish worker, or teach in one of its mission schools.

How many different meanings of the word "church" can you find in this story?
Where do you find reference to the holy Christian Church?
How does Sheryl show a God-pleasing attitude?

FOR DEVOTIONS

A Luther once said this about the Church: "Thank God, a seven-year-old child knows what the Church is, namely holy believers and sheep who hear the voice of their shepherd. So children pray, 'I believe in one holy Christian Church'".

What picture of the Church does Luther use here?
For a different picture of what the Church is like READ 1 Peter 2:4,5.
How does God want to use you in his Church?
What "spiritual sacrifices" could you offer?

B THINK about this story and what it teaches us about our place in the Church. A ship was sailing back to Europe from Africa. Part of its cargo were cages with valuable birds from the African jungle. Out in the middle of the ocean one of the cages was left open. One restless bird, used to being free, escaped and quickly flew far away. For hours it flew over the ocean, glad to be free again. But then it began to grow tired. But it couldn't find anywhere to settle. At last, hours later, the passengers were amazed to see this bird struggling towards the ship on heavy wings. Panting and breathless it settled on the deck. No longer was that ship like a prison, but like a home, a safe refuge.

Why do some people want to "be free" of the Church?
Why are they lost if they turn away from God's family?

READ 1 Peter 2:9,10 to see what it means to belong to God's Church.
Why is the Church the Christian's "home" and a safe place of refuge?

C REPEAT the memory verses, Romans 12:5 and John 8:31,32 and Ephesians 2:19,20 and THINK about what the Holy Christian Church means to you. Thank God for bringing you into his family. Ask him to help you be a faithful member of his Church and to bring you to your eternal home.

FAMILY TIME

READ to your family the question asked by the Hindu visitor (top of page 101 in "Growing...").

Have the family TALK about the various meanings of "church".
READ Ephesians 2:19-22 and close with the Lord's Prayer.

MORE TO DO

The Church is pictured in many different ways in the Bible. Look up the texts in the RSV Bible to find how it is described, and then find the word in the letter puzzle.

Ephesians 2:21
Romans 12:5
1 Peter 5:2
John 15:5
Luke 17:20
Ephesians 3:15
John 10:27
1 Timothy 3:15
1 Corinthians 3:9 (end of sentence)

B	N	W	O	P	R	E	H	T	O	M
B	B	R	A	N	C	H	E	S	H	L
O	U	C	X	K	I	N	G	D	O	M
D	Y	I	K	N	G	B	E	Q	U	K
Y	B	F	L	O	C	K	N	W	S	T
M	V	A	U	D	X	K	L	P	E	S
M	C	M	I	G	I	F	J	M	H	P
L	V	I	D	Q	J	N	P	O	O	U
B	T	L	B	T	Q	L	G	O	L	K
N	B	Y	S	H	E	E	P	G	D	A

25 CHAPTER — FORGIVEN — FULLY AND FREELY

God has forgiven the whole world through the sacrifice of Jesus on the cross. He offers this forgiveness through the means of grace. We receive this gift through faith. We can be quite sure that, for Jesus' sake, God will accept us on Judgment Day as his forgiven people.

READ "GROWING..." pages 105-107.

COMPLETE *the sentences:*

Forgiveness is the _____ gift of God who _____ pardons our sins. When _____ died for the sins of the world, God _____ that all people were _____ for his sake. God _____ us forgiveness through the _____ of the _____ and the _____. We _____ God's forgiveness _____ through _____. We need have no _____ that we are forgiven and that on _____ _____ God will pronounce us _____ _____. Another word for forgiveness is _____ which means to be declared _____. God justifies us by _____ for Christ's _____ through faith.

(justification   receive   sake   doubts   innocent   declared   Christ
faith   preaching   freely   sacraments   personally   Gospel   not guilty
grace   forgiven   offers   undeserved   Judgment Day)

TIME FOR REFLECTION

These people have a wrong understanding of "forgiveness".
WORK OUT *what you could say to them.*

a. Jerry had the bad habit of stealing. When his friend told him that this was wrong and against God's commandments, he replied, "Why should I worry? I can always be forgiven!" ....

b. Mrs. Hughes was a very respectable person who went to church every Sunday and gave a lot of money to charity. The pastor visited her in the hospital when she was sick. He spoke to her about dying. She said, "I'm not scared of dying. God will forgive me. I've lived a good life." ....

c. Stan seldom went to church or to Holy Communion. When the parish worker spoke to him about this he said, "I know I'm forgiven. That's all that matters! Why should I go to church or take Holy Communion?" ....

d. Anne was angry when another girl treated her badly. Soon after this she took part in a devotion and joined in praying for forgiveness. Later when the other girl apologised to her, Anne refused to talk to her or to be her friend again. ....

e. Mr. Turner read in the paper about how some guerilla fighters cruelly treated a Christian missionary and his congregation. "Surely Jesus couldn't have died for those wicked men," he told his wife. ....

FOR DEVOTIONS

A Long ago there was a king who grew very angry with his wife when she did him wrong. He told her that he never wanted to see her again. "If you come into my presence I will have you put to death," he said. The queen was sad and downhearted. Then she had a happy thought. Taking with her the little prince, their only son, she went to the king. Holding the child in her arms she asked the king to forgive her. When the king heard her say this and saw the prince in her arms, he straight away went over to her and kissed her.

Why did the king forgive the queen?
READ 1 Peter 2:22-25 and think about how God forgives you for the sake of his Son.

B A kind doctor worked among some very poor people who often didn't have the money to pay him. So he would write over his accounts in red ink, "FORGIVEN". When he died, lawyers went to court to try to have these accounts paid. But when the judge examined the doctor's books and saw what he had written, he gave his judgment, "Payment of these accounts has been cancelled!"

SAY the memory verses Ephesians 1:7 and Romans 5:8 and think about how God has written "FORGIVEN" over your sins. Thank God for forgiving you.

C Little Jamie had a row with his playmate. "I'm never going to play with you again," he yelled. But next morning he went out to play with his friend again as though nothing had happened. "I thought you weren't going to play with Fred again," his mother asked with a smile. Jamie didn't know what to say at first, but then he gave a grin and said, "Oh, Fred and me's good forgetters!"

What can you learn from little Jamie?
READ Micah 7:18-20 to discover what God does with your sins. Ask God to help you to be forgiving to others.

FAMILY TIME

Show your family the illustrations on pages 105-107 of "Growing..." and talk about God's forgiveness. Discuss why it is so important that members of the family freely forgive each other. READ 1 Peter 2:22-25. Close by reading or singing hymn 330, Lutheran Hymnal: "Rock of ages".

MORE TO DO

These three hearts tell the story of God's forgiveness. Decode the message to find out the colour of the hearts and their meaning.

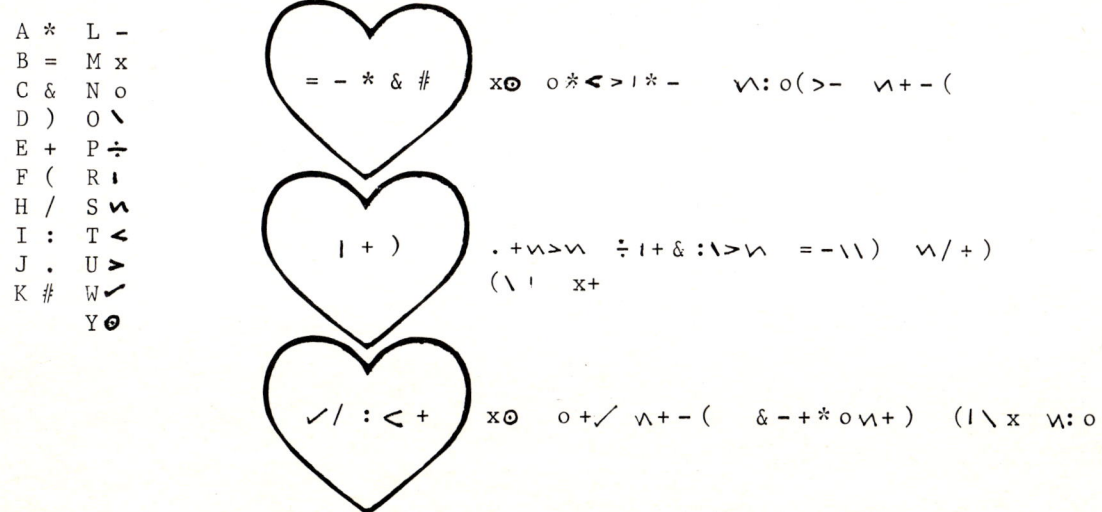

CHAPTER 26 — OUR SURE HOPE

Because all people are sinners they must die. But Christians need not fear death because Jesus has taken away its sting. When they die they go to be with Jesus. Death is like a sleep from which God will awaken us when he raises us up with glorified bodies on the day of resurrection, and takes us to live with him for ever in heaven.

READ "GROWING..." pages 109-111.

THINK about these questions:

1. Why are people usually afraid of dying?
2. What comforts a Christian when he faces death?
3. What will happen to believers on the day of resurrection?
4. What is meant by "eternal death"?
5. How does the Bible describe heaven?

TIME FOR REFLECTION

FIND the sentence which best describes the attitude of these people:

a. As Mr. Brown lay dying in hospital he was not afraid because he knew that Jesus had taken his sins away.

b. As Mr. Adams grew older he was often depressed because he believed that death was the end and there was nothing to hope for.

c. The Hindu felt it was silly to worry about God's judgment because he thought he would be born again and again in other lives.

d. Old Mr. Johnson often talked to his little grandson about Jesus. He especially liked to tell him about heaven.

e. Barry was only 10 years old. He knew he was dying from a serious illness. He told his mother not to cry and said, "I'm going to be with Jesus".

... He often thought about his heavenly home.

... He knew he was safe in Jesus' care.

... He had no hope of eternal life.

... He trusted firmly that God had forgiven him for Jesus' sake.

... He did not believe in Judgment Day.

FOR DEVOTIONS

A It was the custom among some of the early Christians not to wail and lament when a fellow believer died. Instead they held a joyful service and spoke of the Christian's death as his "birthday" - the day when he had gone to be with the Lord to begin a new life in heaven.

Why did they call a Christian's death his "birthday"?

READ Romans 14:7-9. Why can't death separate you from Jesus your Lord?

B THINK about these words by a Christian writer.

What does it mean for the Christian to die and be raised again? It is like an ugly bulb being planted in the ground and springing up in new form as a beautiful white lily. It is like a caterpillar which goes through the cocoon stage coming forth as a colourful butterfly. It is like the sun setting in the west in darkness and coming up with bright new light in the east. It is like going to sleep sick and tired out and waking up in the morning a new person, filled with God's own life.

READ 1 Corinthians 15:42-56 and THINK about what it means for you that one day you will rise from the dead.

B One of the best things about heaven is that Jesus will be there! One writer tells us what this means to him:

The light of heaven is Jesus' face; the joy of heaven is Jesus being with us; the music of heaven is singing praise to Jesus; the news in heaven is the work of Jesus; our work in heaven is serving Jesus; the fulness of heaven is the Lord Jesus himself!

READ St. John's description of heaven in Revelation 21:22 - 22:5. WRITE a paragraph with the title, "What Heaven Will Be Like". PRAY to God, thanking him for giving you this wonderful hope and asking him to keep you safely in his family until he takes you to your heavenly home.

FAMILY TIME

You could READ "God Gives Eternal Life" from page 111 of "Growing..." and have the family TALK about how they imagine heaven will be. Then READ Revelation 21:22 - 22:5. CLOSE with a prayer thanking God for giving us this hope. If you have written a paragraph about heaven read this to the family.

MORE TO DO

Write three short paragraphs saying what the Three Articles of the Creed mean to you.

UNIT THREE: THE LORD'S PRAYER

27 CHAPTER — SPEAKING TO OUR FATHER

God invites us to speak to him in prayer because he is our Father and we are his children through Jesus. So, we talk to him confidently in Jesus' name knowing that he has promised to hear and answer us. We worship God in prayer as we show our trust in him and give him thanks and praise. Jesus has taught us how to pray in the Lord's Prayer.

READ "GROWING..." pages 113-115.

CONNECT the endings to the right sentences:

1. We talk to God as our Father ... and also because he has promised to hear us and we need his help and blessing.

2. Prayer is an act of worship ... there are special times and places when we should pray.

3. We pray because of God's command ... but also for the needs of others.

4. To pray in Jesus' name means ... because we are his children through Jesus.

5. We can pray at any time but ... but in the way he knows is best for us.

6. We are to pray not only for our own needs ... through which we express our faith in God and give him praise.

7. We can expect God to answer us ... that we go to our Father through the Saviour.

TIME FOR REFLECTION

FIND a sentence from pages 114, 115 of "Growing..." which could help these people in their attitude to prayer.

a. Brent and his sister were hurt in an accident. As he lay in hospital Brent kept asking God to make him better, but he seldom thought of including his sister.

b. A pious Moslem prayed a long prayer to Allah but didn't mention the name of Jesus.

c. Tom was worried about some tests at school. His mother encouraged him to talk to God about it, but Tim didn't think this was important enough to pray about.

d. Brenda asked God to help her overcome her bad temper, but the next time she lost her temper she decided it was no use and gave up praying about it.

e. Bob often prayed the Lord's Prayer when he went to bed at night, but usually he was not thinking about what the words really meant.

FOR DEVOTIONS

A READ what a modern writer tells us about praying to God.

"I like to think that there is an invisible telephone line stretching between my Father's heavenly home and me. Every day as soon as possible, I like to take off the receiver and speak to my Father. I know that he is always at the other end of the line and ready to hear and answer me because Jesus has told me so. After saying, 'Dear Father in heaven', I first of all like to praise him and thank him for listening to me and for all he has done for me. Then I simply tell him what I want to say: about my own life and about others who need help. As I say 'Amen', peace fills my heart and I am full of joy. I know that God will never leave me and is present to help me through the day. Truly, I could not get through the day without prayer!"

READ Philippians 4:4-7. THINK about how your life can be full of joy and peace as you speak to your heavenly Father in prayer.

B Our prayers for others are a good way of showing what is our own relationship to God. Why?

READ Matthew 15:21-28. What can we learn about this Canaanite woman from her prayer? Do you ever feel that God is not answering your prayers? Why was this woman sure that Jesus would answer her? Why is she a fine example for you?

C WRITE your own prayer in the space below. TALK to God about your daily life.

FAMILY TIME

Your family could draw up a list of people and needs for which to pray together during the week. For a devotion READ Philippians 4:4-7, use your own prayer and sing together the hymn "What a friend we have in Jesus" (Lutheran Hymnal 426). A family member might like to help you make a poster entitled:

WHY WORRY WHEN YOU CAN PRAY?

MORE TO DO

WRITE your own prayer about your daily life.

ADDRESS GOD

PRAISE GOD

CONFESS TO GOD

THANK GOD

ASK GOD

COME TO GOD THROUGH JESUS

28 CHAPTER
FIRST THINGS FIRST

In the Lord's Prayer Jesus encourages us first of all to pray for God's name and kingdom and that his will may be done. First, we ask God to help us keep his name holy and lead others to praise him. Then we think of how God rules in our lives with his grace. We request God to keep us in his kingdom and to bring others into his family. Because powerful enemies are opposed to God we pray that his will may be done. We ask him to help us fight against evil and live as his people.

READ "GROWING..." pages 117-119. If the following statements are true, circle the first letter. If false, circle the second letter.

G X   Jesus wants us to pray first of all for God's honour and glory.
O F   To hallow God's name means that we want to keep his name holy.
B D   Because God's name is holy in itself it doesn't matter much how we live.
I F   God's rule of grace comes to us through Jesus.
H S   We should not pray for God's kingdom to come because it comes of itself.
H P   God's kingdom comes when people believe his Word and live as his people.
T O   God's will includes what he wants to do for us but not what he wants us to do for him.
N L   If we live holy lives God will not let suffering come to us.
M Y   If we try hard enough we can do God's will perfectly on earth, like the angels in heaven.

TIME FOR REFLECTION

FIND references to the first three petitions in this story and how they applied to Charlie's life that day.

Charlie felt rather depressed as he went to college that day. "Why can't I control my temper?" he thought. That morning he had had a row with his older brother. He had lost his temper and let fly with bad language which caused his brother to join in. Dad had heard them and had angrily told them to stop. "Do you really think that kind of language is right for Christians?" he asked. "Well," thought Charlie, "at least I apologised before I left home!"

The chapel devotion made him feel better. The chaplain told them about a missionary of the church who was working among the heathen in a foreign country. "God has called us all to be his witnesses," the pastor told the students. "God, help me be a better witness at home," Charlie prayed silently. "I really do want to be a Christian, but my bad temper gets me into trouble. Help me keep control of myself next time Frank bugs me! I know what you want me to do. Help me to do it." Praying like this helped Charlie. He even joined in singing a Gospel song. Lessons that day didn't seem so bad. In a Scripture lesson he was able to help another boy understand something from the Bible. "Thanks, Father, for making me a member of your family," he thought as he went to bed that night.

FOR DEVOTIONS

A This missionary story can help you understand what it means to hallow God's name and help his kingdom come.

An African told the missionary in his village that he wanted to become a Christian. "But you've never been to our church services or been taught the Gospel," the missionary replied. "No, but I've seen the Gospel and I want to be a Christian, too," the African replied. The missionary and other Christians were living examples of Jesus. By their lives they helped draw this man to his Saviour.

READ Acts 4:5-12. *How does Peter hallow God's name? How is he helping God's kingdom to come?*

THINK *about how you can be a witness for Christ.*

B "It's not that I don't know what to do. My problem is being able to do it!" a young Christian complained. That's a problem all of us face. We need to receive strength daily to carry out God's will. Jesus is our great example here: "My food is to do the will of him who sent me," he told his disciples. Daily we need to ask God to give us his Spirit so that we may try to do his will like Jesus.

READ *Jesus' own prayer in John 17:11-19.* *How did Jesus do his Father's will? How did he hallow God's name and make his kingdom come?*

WRITE *a prayer based on one of these petitions, asking God to make you more like Jesus.*

C REPEAT *the memory verse Matthew 5:16 and THINK about how you can let your light shine.* As you REPEAT *1 Timothy 2:4* THINK *of a friend* who is not a Christian and put his/her name in the place of "all men". Then ask God to help you witness to that person.

FAMILY TIME

Could your family befriend someone who has not yet come into God's kingdom? TALK *about* this together and how you might be able to help the person find Jesus. For your devotion you could READ the story about the African and the missionary, followed by Acts 4:5-12. If you wrote a prayer, use this to close the devotion.

MORE TO DO

These words describe what salt and light do: unscramble them and put them under the right headings.
Write down one thing you will try to do: as salt; as light.

iisreufp   nssieh   disueg   sreevespr   vlsreae   sonsaes

SALT	LIGHT
....	....
....	....
....	....
Jesus wants me to be like salt. I will:	Jesus wants me to let my light shine. I will:

29 CHAPTER

NO WORRIES!

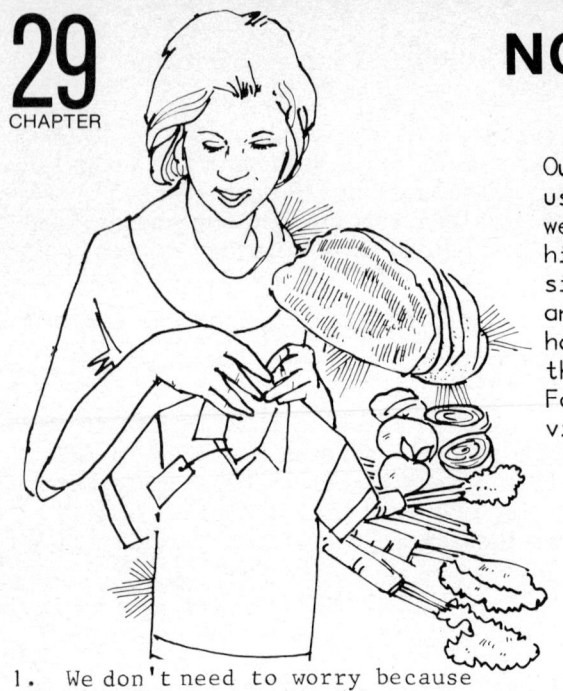

Our heavenly Father promises to care for us - so we ask him to provide us with what we need for daily life. He has shown us his mercy in Jesus - so we confess our sins, ask him to forgive us for Jesus' sake and promise to forgive other people who have done wrong to us. By praying like this we leave all our worries with our Father and show that we trust him to provide for us in body and soul.

READ "GROWING..." pages 121-123.

COMPLETE these sentences:

1. We don't need to worry because

2. Daily bread means

3. We ask for DAILY bread because

4. We confess our sins to God because

5. We tell God that we will forgive others because

TIME FOR REFLECTION

WRITE down how people in these stories show good attitudes. FIND a text from pages 121-123 of "Growing..." which applies to each example.

a. Mr. Gregory lost his job when his firm sacked many of the workers. He kept on looking for work but was not very successful. His wife got more and more worried. "However can we live just on unemployment benefits," she asked. "I'm sure I'll find a job," Mr. Gregory replied. "We know our heavenly Father cares for us."
   ....

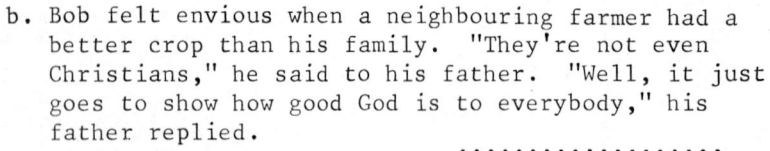

b. Bob felt envious when a neighbouring farmer had a better crop than his family. "They're not even Christians," he said to his father. "Well, it just goes to show how good God is to everybody," his father replied.
   ....

c. Mary felt disgusted with herself. She knew she shouldn't have said bad things about her friend, and what was worse, she had told a lie when her friend spoke to her about it. "I'm sorry that I do these wrong things," she told God in her prayers. "Forgive me and help me do better."
   ....

d. Bill got very angry when someone treated him badly. "You wait, I'll get even with him," he threatened. "Why don't you try being kind to him instead," his friend suggested. "He may be sorry that he treated you like that."
   ....

FOR DEVOTIONS

A Many years ago Pastor Francke founded a home in Halle, Germany, to care for orphans. He trusted in God to care for his work. He tells how again and again, when he had no food or money left for the children, God heard his prayers for help. He writes, "Once all our food was gone. As I prayed the Lord's Prayer that day I found myself especially thinking about the words of the Fourth Petition, "this day", because we really needed God's help that particular day. While I was still praying, a friend knocked on my door and brought me $1000. This kept us going for weeks. How good God is to us."

READ James 5:16-18. God hears your prayers and cares for you daily.
THINK of how he has cared for your needs today. THANK him for this.

B *READ 1 Kings 17:8-16 and THINK about* how God provides for us today through the miracle of seeds, crops and the fertility of nature. Find some prayers which are suitable for table grace and use them at meal-time this week. (For example, hymns 635-641, Lutheran Hymnal.)

C A cruel slavemaster often used to make fun of his Christian slave. "What can Jesus do for you now," he asked the slave one day mockingly, as he was about to whip him. "He can teach me to forgive you, massa," was the reply.

READ Matthew 5:38-45 and THINK about what Jesus says. Has anyone wronged you recently? *Why should you forgive this person. How can v 45 help you do this?*
Thank God for forgiving you and ask him to help you forgive others.

FAMILY TIME

As a devotion with your family you could *READ* the sections, "We Confess our Sins", "Father Forgive Us" and "As We Forgive", from page 123 of "Growing...". Then you could *READ Psalm 103:8-14* and the family could *DISCUSS* the statement "We don't need to worry about our sins". Close with the Lord's Prayer.

MORE TO DO

Complete the hymn verses by filling in the right words. (You will find these verses in hymn 421, Lutheran Hymnal.)

| Our Father thou in heaven above,
Who biddest us to dwell in ....
As members of one family,
And cry for all we need to ....
Grant that no idle words we say,
But from our heart sincerely ..... | Forgive our trespasses, we pray;
Take all their burdening guilt ....,
As we their trespasses forgive
Who us by their offences ......,
Thus let us dwell in charity
And serve each other ....

Amen, that is, So shall it be,
Confirm our faith and hope in ....,
That we may doubt not, but believe
What here we ask we shall ....
Thus in thy name and at thy word
We say: Amen, O hear us, ... |

CHAPTER 30 — WINNING THE FINAL VICTORY

We need God's help to overcome our spiritual enemies. We ask our Father to keep us from being tempted and to help us win the victory when we are tempted. We turn to God in our need, asking him to set us free from evil, to help us in time of trouble, and to take us to our heavenly home. Finally, in the Lord's Prayer, we praise our powerful, glorious Father and express our confidence that he hears us, by saying "Amen!"

READ "GROWING..." pages 125-127.

CORRECT these sentences:

1. God tempts people to sin by letting troubles come into their lives.
2. God uses times of testing to draw us away from him.
3. Although we need God's help we must overcome temptations by ourselves.
4. Death is too horrible to be a blessing, even for Christians.
5. God will keep all troubles and suffering from us provided we believe in him firmly enough.
6. We can't be certain that God will answer our prayers because there is so much evil in the world.
7. We say "Amen" to make sure God will hear and answer us.

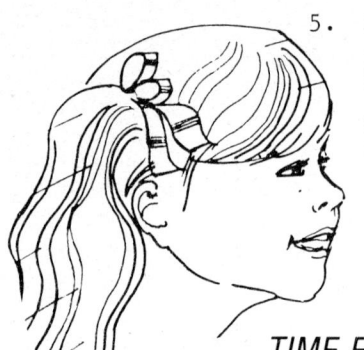

TIME FOR REFLECTION

COMPLETE the sentences:

a. Brenton asked God to help him when he was tempted...
b. Dave stopped going out with some friends who got involved in drug-taking...
c. Jean felt sorry and ashamed that she had cheated in a test...
d. After Don was rescued from the sea after a boating accident...
e. When Mrs. Jones experienced much trouble and suffering...
f. Although Mr. Lynch felt sad when his wife died after a long illness...
g. Sheryl joined a church choir...

... so she asked God to help her not to do it again.
... he praised God for setting her free from all her troubles.
... she asked God to help her bear it patiently.
... because he felt that he couldn't depend on his own strength.
... because she wanted to join in singing God's praise.
... because he thought he might be tempted to join in.
... he felt very thankful to God for preserving his life.

FOR DEVOTIONS

A An ancient Greek legend tells how Achilles' mother dipped him as a baby in the waters of the River Styx so that he could never be killed. Every spot on his body was protected - except for his heel, by which his mother had held him when she dipped him in the magic waters. Achilles became a famous warrior and couldn't be harmed - until an arrow shot by Paris struck his heel and poisoned him so that he died.

This legend can teach you something about the danger of temptation.
READ Matthew 18:7-9. Jesus tells us to be on our guard against our "weak spots" through which the devil may tempt us.
What are your "weak spots"? How can God guard you against them?

B A little boy was looking at a pile of beautiful apples outside a fruit shop. The shop-keeper noticed how he was looking at them. Coming up to him he said, "I hope you're not trying to take any of my apples!" "No, sir!" the boy replied. "I'm trying NOT to take one."

What did the boy mean?

It is important that we try to avoid temptation wherever possible.
READ 2 Thessalonians 3:3-5 and THINK about how God promises to guard you from evil.

C READ Psalm 27. The psalmwriter trusts God to deliver him from evil.
Find or underline verses which tell you this. You could READ hymn 400 in the Lutheran Hymnal to see how the hymnwriter speaks in a way similar to this psalmist.

D WRITE the Lord's Prayer in your own words (see below). Plan to use this prayer for a family devotion. Make your own prayer list and use this as a guide for your praying.

FAMILY TIME

Have the family share experiences of how God has preserved them from dangers to: the body; the soul; property.
Use Psalm 27:1-6 and the Lord's Prayer in your own words for a devotion. The family could READ or SING the hymn, "A mighty fortress" (Lutheran Hymnal, 195).

MORE TO DO

Write in what the various parts of the armour of God stand for. You can discover this from Ephesians 6:10-17.

WRITE THE LORD'S PRAYER IN YOUR OWN WORDS:

Introduction

Seven Petitions
1
2
3
4
5
6
7

Conclusion

CHAPTER 31

UNIT FOUR: HOLY BAPTISM
GOD GIVES NEW LIFE

Holy Baptism is the means God used to bring us his grace so that we experienced new birth as his children. Through the Sacrament of water connected with God's Word, we received the Holy Spirit and were made believers. In this way God made us members in his family, the Church, so that we now have a personal relationship with him as his children. Jesus commanded his disciples to baptize all people, including infants.

READ "GROWING..." pages 129-131.

FIT the words into their right places.

congregation   Baptism   God's Word   grace   infants
members   pouring   Triune   miracle   children   water
sinful   church   name   washing   work   new birth
Sacrament   forgiveness

To be born as a child of God is a _____ of God's _____. God gives this _____ through _____. Holy Baptism is a _____ in which _____ is used together with _____. God is at ____ in Baptism making us his own _____. In Baptism water is applied in the ____ of the ____ God. Water may be used in various ways, such as by _____ or _____. Baptism is also for _____ because they are born _____ and need _____. Through Baptism we become _____ of God's _____ and join a Christian _____.

TIME FOR REFLECTION

God is at work in your life through Baptism. THINK about this as you READ the sentences and then WRITE down how they make you feel.

Through Baptism:

a. God promises to be my God and to keep me safe in his hands. _____
b. God has forgiven me my sins and accepted me as his child. _____
c. God shows me how much I need his help and blessing. _____
d. God came and claimed me as his own and didn't wait for me to find him. _____
e. God shows me that he is faithful and that I can rely on him. _____
f. I have a special kind of relationship with God as a member of his family. _____

FOR DEVOTIONS

A King Louis the Pious of France once said, "The three handfuls of water that were poured over my head in Holy Baptism are worth more to me than the crown I am wearing". *Why did the king say this?*

   READ Ephesians 2:1-6. How does the apostle describe the life of unbelievers? THINK about what it means for you that you have been born anew and are now a child of God.

B READ Galatians 3:25-29.

"What does it mean to put on Christ? It is certainly not like putting on a new set of clothes which you can take off again at night, or merely 'turning over a new leaf'. It is far more than this. It means nothing less than being born a new person. You are no longer just your old sinful self. Now, through the Spirit, you are a new self - a person who has put on Christ's holiness and way of life, his Spirit and power. That is what it means to 'put on Christ'. All that and more!"

THINK about what the writer says and how it applies to your own life.

C Through Baptism you have received the name of the Triune God.
   ... God is your Father: thank him for making you his child and for caring for you day by day;
   ... God is your Saviour: ask Jesus to help you be his faithful follower;
   ... God is your Sanctifier: ask the Spirit to fill you with his power so that you may live as a child of God.

FAMILY TIME

You could have a family devotion centering on your Baptism. LOOK at your baptismal certificate and TALK about when, where and by whom you were baptized. ASK your parents about their Baptism. If you have brothers or sisters look at their certificates also. READ Acts 2:37-42 and close with a prayer to the Triune God as suggested in part C above.

MORE TO DO

Think about your Baptism as you work out the crossword.

CLUES:

Across:
3. How the sacred act of Baptism may be described.
5. Those whom Jesus also wants to be baptized.
9. One way in which water can be applied in Baptism.
11. The local community of Christians which we join when we are baptized.
13. What God offers and gives us through Baptism.

Down:
1. Another way in which water can be applied in Baptism.
2. The persons who normally baptize.
3. People who witness a Baptism and speak for the child.
4. What God gives you through Baptism.
6. God's gift in Baptism through which we receive his promises.
7. The kind of relationship which we have with God through Baptism.
8. God's family in which we become members through Baptism.
10. The words Jesus commanded us to use in Baptism tell us this.
12. The one who commanded us to Baptize.

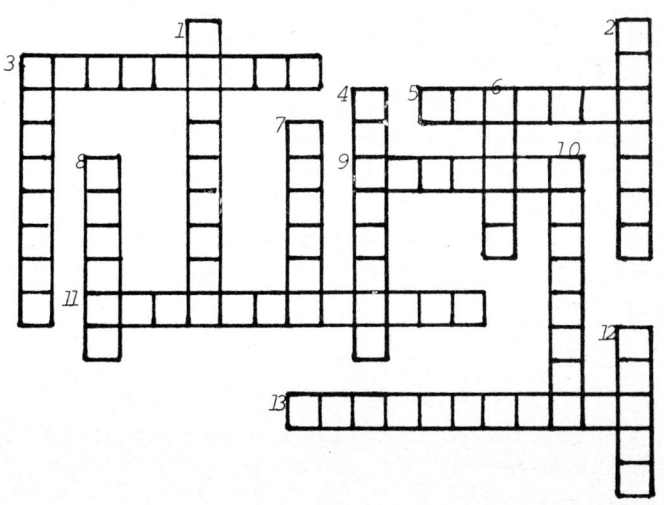

CHAPTER 32
BLESSING AND POWER FOR GROWTH

God brings us great blessings through Baptism. He forgives us our sins, sets us free from our enemies and gives us everlasting life. God's Word gives Baptism its power so that we receive these blessings through faith. Through Baptism God makes his covenant with us and adopts us as his children. God remains faithful to his promises for ever.

READ "GROWING..." pages 133-135.

MARK these sentences True or False:

1. ...God uses water in a special way in the Sacrament of Baptism.
2. ...Because Jesus paid for our sins by dying for us we don't really need to be baptized.
3. ...Although God has set us free from sin, the devil still has us under his power.
4. ...Through Baptism we share in Jesus' victory over death.
5. ...God's Word with water gives Baptism its power to bless us.
6. ...By nature we are all the children of God.
7. ...God's covenant with us is his solemn agreement to be our gracious God for ever.

TIME FOR REFLECTION

WORK OUT what you would say to these people. You may find statements from "Growing..." which can help you.

a. Mr. Lloyd was discussing Baptism with his friend. "It's silly to think that sprinkling a few drops of water on someone's head and saying a few words can make any difference," the friend commented.

b. As the confirmation class was learning about the blessings of Baptism, Shane remarked, "I can see how God forgives our sins through Baptism, but I can't see how it delivers from death. We all still die, don't we?"

c. Andrea joined a group to take part in occult practices. When her Christian friend warned her against doing this, Andrea replied, "The devil can't hurt me. I've been baptized."

d. Mrs. Hanson brought her baby to the pastor to arrange for his Baptism. "I must get my baby baptized," she thought, "otherwise he might have an accident or be harmed in some way."

e. When Mrs. Gordon's little boy kept playing up she was angry with him. "Behave yourself, Johnny," she scolded, "else God will punish you. Jesus doesn't like naughty little boys."

FOR DEVOTIONS

A *What does it mean that through Baptism God gives you faith to receive his blessings?* Read what this writer says about it:

"In Baptism God gives us the faith that goes with his promises. He says to us, 'You're not guilty; you're one of mine and worth keeping forever.....All I have is yours and I've given it to you in your Baptism as a gift. All I want is to make a believer out of you. And I'm doing that myself. I'm making you what I want you to be. I started in your Baptism and I'm going to keep at it until the day I take you to myself.' "   *(Free To Be, p. 167,168)*

READ Ephesians 2:4-10. THINK about all that God does for you through Baptism.

B REPEAT the memory texts Acts 22:16 and Galatians 3:26,27 and THINK about how you experience the blessings of Baptism.

Here is what a Christian writer says about the blessings of Baptism: "What a marvellous treasure Baptism is! Just think what God has done for us through its power. We were blind - now we can see; we were dead in sin - now we are alive; we were lost - now we are found; we were slaves of Satan - now we are the free children of God. Indeed, at our Baptism, God began to pour into our lives all the blessings he planned for us through Jesus. For our part, let's appreciate this precious gift and thank God daily for all he has done and still does for us through this washing of life."

C "Baptism is like an adoption ceremony." Why? THINK of what adoption means for a child: a new name; new parents; a new family; a whole new life, and usually, love and security.
READ Galatians 4:4-7 and THINK about what it means for YOU to be adopted as God's child.

FAMILY TIME

Your family may like to help you design and make a poster entitled "BAPTISM SAVES US". Display it in your home.
As a devotion you could read "God's Word has Special Power" and "Adopted by God" from "Growing..." page 135. READ Galatians 3:26-27 and close with a prayer thanking God for the blessings of Baptism.

MORE TO DO

Unscramble the words:

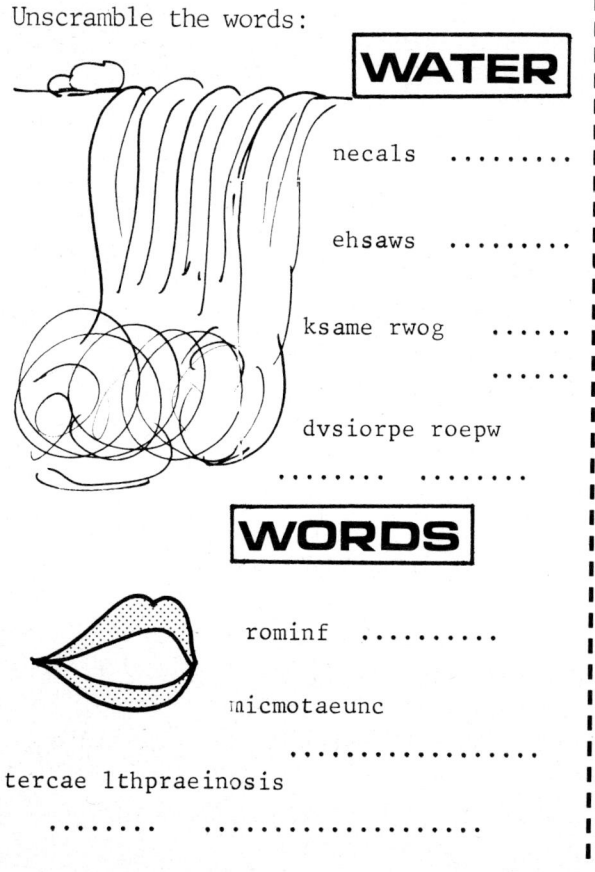

WATER

necals ....

ehsaws ....

ksame rwog ......
....

dvsiorpe roepw
....

WORDS

rominf ....

micmotaeunc
....

tercae lthpraeinosis
....

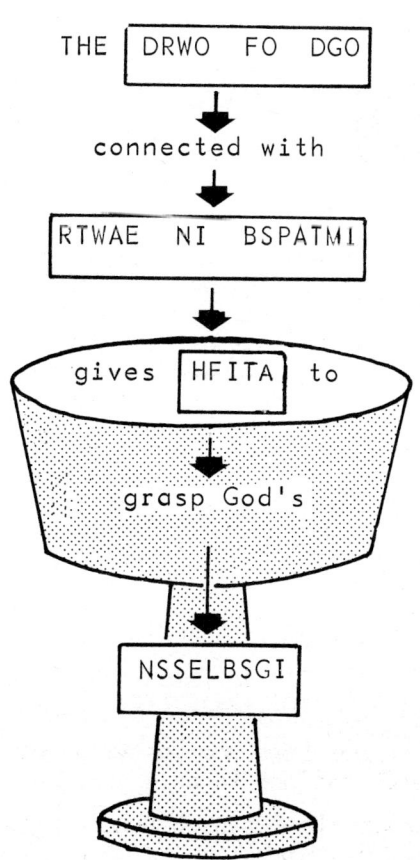

THE DRWO FO DGO

connected with

RTWAE NI BSPATMI

gives HFITA to

grasp God's

NSSELBSGI

CHAPTER 33 — POWER TO LIVE AS GOD'S CHILD

Baptism means that we died to sin and came alive as children of God. God calls us to live in the grace and power of our Baptism as we struggle against our old sinful self and live in newness of life. Because we are baptized the Holy Spirit works in us, leading us to daily repentance and strengthening us to live holy lives as God's people. Baptism encourages us to keep on growing and living as God's children. It makes us sure that we are God's, and that nothing can separate us from our Father's love.

READ "GROWING..." pages 137-139.

THINK about these questions and then write short answers:

1. Why is it such a struggle for us to live as children of God?
2. What does it mean that in Baptism we 'died to sin'?
3. What does it mean that we 'rose to new life'?
4. What is meant by daily repentance?
5. How does our Baptism comfort and encourage us?

TIME FOR REFLECTION

THE UPS AND DOWNS OF LIFE

Tim felt miserable as he walked home from his friend's place. He had been having a good time with Bob, listening to cassettes and talking. But the enjoyable time had ended in a fight. Bob had started teasing him about a girl-friend. "Why did I have to get mad at him?" thought Tim. "I know he was only joking."

When he got home he sat in the loungeroom watching TV. Presently his two younger sisters began quarrelling. Tim talked to them and was able to help them make the peace again. His mother noticed what he had done and told him she was pleased he had helped.

As Tim had his evening devotion he thought about the day. "What sort of person am I anyway," he wondered. "One moment I'm fighting, the next I'm helping others to stop fighting!" As he read his Bible and thought about how God loved him, he felt thankful that he was a Christian. "Thanks for forgiving me when I go wrong, God," he prayed. "Help me live your way." Then he thought of his fight with Bob. "I'm sorry about that," he told God. He made up his mind to apologise as soon as he saw Bob next day.

As you read this story underline references to:

...the old sinful self;   ...the new nature God gives;   ...how Tim 'died to sin';   ...how he came 'alive to God';   ...what is meant by daily repentance.

FOR DEVOTIONS

A The first of the famous 95 Theses (which Luther nailed to the church in Wittenberg in 1517) reads like this:

"When our Lord and Master Jesus Christ says 'repent' he wants the whole life of his Christians to be a constant repentance."

Compare this with what Luther teaches in the explanation of the Catechism, Baptism, part 4.

READ Psalm 130. THINK about what it means for you to die to sin and come alive for God day by day.

B   Here is what one writer says about the daily drowning of the old sinful self and daily rising of the new self.

" 'Remember your Baptism', the Spirit says. As the Old Adam fights and struggles, remember what God did when you were baptized - how he promised to make you, a crying baby, one of his own, to make you new and to bring you into his new creation to dwell with him. Through the Word and Sacraments the Spirit will give you faith day by day and keep you in it. God sent his Spirit to kill the Old Adam in you and to raise up the new you day by day. You can be sure God will do it! He keeps his promises. It's for certain!"
('Free To Be', page 175.)

READ Romans 8:12-17 and see what the apostle says about this.

C   "Try standing in one place on a bicycle and you'll soon fall over. You can keep upright only by pedalling onwards. So it is with your Christian life. God keeps us as his own people by leading us along the way of Christian growth and experience."

In *Philippians 3:12-17* the apostle Paul tells you about his goal in life. Ask God to keep leading you along his way and to help you grow and mature as a Christian.

FAMILY TIME

Here are some ideas for helping you to remember your Baptism and to think about it in your daily life. TALK about these with your family and decide which of them you could do.

...having a special celebration on the date of your Baptism;   ...inviting your sponsors to visit you on that date;   ...talking about the facts recorded on your Baptism certificate;   ...displaying the certificate in your room.
Can you think of others?

As a devotion you could READ "Remember Your Baptism" ("Growing..." page 138), Romans 8:12-17 and then READ or SING the hymn, "O Jesus I have promised", (Lutheran Hymnal 371).

MORE TO DO

Here are a number of ways you can show your thankfulness to God for making you his child through Baptism and keeping you safe in his family. Tick those which you intend to carry out with God's help.

	✓		✓
Attend church regularly		Make time for a daily devotion	
Take part in a Bible study group		Speak up for Jesus among your friends	
Speak well of other people		Keep the peace in family life	
Avoid bad language		Consider becoming a church worker	
Pray for the work of God's church		Do your school work faithfully	
Have a loving relationship with family members		Set a good example in your group	
Avoid unclean thoughts		Willingly do your share of household chores	

34 CHAPTER
UNIT FIVE: HOLY COMMUNION
INVITED TO THE FEAST

The Sacrament of the Altar, or the Lord's Supper, is the sacred meal which Jesus instituted for his church on the night before he died. In the Lord's Supper, Jesus gives his body and blood in and with bread and wine for us to eat and to drink. In this sacrament we remember that Jesus died for us and offered himself as a sacrifice for the forgiveness of sins. Jesus invites us to this feast of God's family and gives us his grace and blessing.

READ "GROWING..." pages 141-143.

COMPLETE *this lettergram:*

Letters	Clue
_ _ _ L _ _	Jesus is ..... present in the Lord's Supper.
_ _ O _ _	Together with the wine Jesus gives us his .....
_ _ _ R _ _ _ _	Jesus gave this sacrament the night he was ....
_ _ D _	Together with the bread Jesus gives us his ....
_ _ _ S _	Jesus invites us to this wonderful .....
_ _ _ _ _ _ S	The Lord's Supper is for repentant ....
_ _ _ _ _ _ U _ _ _	The Lord's Supper was .... by Christ.
_ _ _ P _ _	The Eucharist is another name for the Lord's ......
_ _ P _ _ _ _ _	The bread and wine do not just .... the body and blood of Christ.
_ _ _ E _	Jesus told us to use bread and ....
_ _ _ _ _ _ R	At the Lord's Supper we .... the Lord's death.

TIME FOR REFLECTION

WRITE down what you would say to these people.

a. Fred said that he didn't need to go to the Lord's Supper because he already had the forgiveness of sins by believing in Jesus.

b. Jane doubted whether Jesus could really be present at the Lord's Supper. "How can he be in all the places where the Lord's Supper is being celebrated at the same time?" she thought.

c. Robert didn't go to Holy Communion because he thought he was too sinful.

These people have a good attitude to the Sacrament. WRITE down why.

a. Gwen went to the Lord's Supper regularly. "Receiving the body and blood of Jesus makes me sure that he died for me," she thought.

b. Tom was glad to receive the Sacrament. "Going to Holy Communion helps me in my troubles," he said, "because I can share in Jesus' victory over sin."

c. As old Mrs. Herbert joined with the congregation in the Lord's Supper she thought how wonderful it will be to share in Christ's victory feast in heaven with all God's people.

FOR DEVOTIONS

A Your friend invites you to a party so that you can share your friendship and enjoy each other's company and the food and drink provided. Think of the great honour Jesus does us in Holy Communion. He invites us to his supper as our Friend, to have fellowship with him and to share in the wonderful blessings he gives us. Surely there is no greater treasure than this holy feast!

READ Matthew 11:28-30 and THINK about what this invitation of the Lord Jesus means for you.

B READ 1 Corinthians 10:16,17. THINK about the two important teachings of Paul here, and what they mean for you.

v. 17: Many separate grains of wheat are ground into flour and used to bake one loaf of bread. So, in Holy Communion we all share in the same bread because we, though many, are joined together into the one body of Christ.

v. 16: In the Lord's Supper Jesus gives us his body and blood to eat and drink united with the bread and wine in a wonderful way which we cannot fully understand. In this way he unites himself with us as our Saviour.

C REPEAT the memory verses 1Corinthians 10:16; 11:26. READ hymn 292 (Lutheran Hymnal), 'The death of Christ', and THINK about what it teaches. Use v. 6 as your prayer.

FAMILY TIME

Perhaps the family will help you prepare a poster about Holy Communion. Display it in your home.
TALK to the family about what Holy Communion is and what it means. Then, as a devotion, READ "The Gracious Host", and "The Wonderful Feast" ("Growing..." page 142). You could close the devotion by reading the hymn "The death of Christ" (Lutheran Hymnal 292).

MORE TO DO

In the lettergram find various names for the Lord's Supper referred to on page 142 of "Growing...".

```
S L P N V H D J P U R E S C M L M X W
J A C X F L P Y H B V D K L P O N V D
H L C M B C H L P Y T Q A G K R L N C
F L N R V N M K L D R T U I M D L P F
S M L K A F H J O D F O P L P S N V X
M L P H G M J H R G K L P D E S W C L
O M K H G C E O D L H J V C I U R Q X
K M L B V X Z N S F D J K Y R P P U I
D L U T G C K O T O P N B C X P Z Q W
E K L J N B V C A O O U T E T E P Y R
U L U T C F T B B P F Y T Y V R N P W
C M K L U T C B L M P T Y I F V N M Y
H L M K L G V I E R U O H B I K M V R
A L J O B V U I F B Y I B E O P B U C
R L P B N U R C B U I N V M A S S O R
I I Y U V R U O P B C N U T E L Y P V
S V Y I P K N M B C Y V N O G B T I T
T M O B U V F R Y I N B C B N I Y A R
H O L Y C O M M U N I O N I M B F R R
```

Unscramble the words to discover what the pastor sometimes says as he invites members of the congregation to come to the Lord's Supper:

OCME   ROF   LAL   GHSNTI

REA   WON   DAYRE.

CHAPTER 35 — FOR YOU!

In the Lord's Supper Jesus assures each of us personally that he died for us. His words, "This is my body and blood, given and shed for you", give power to the Sacrament. We receive the great blessings of forgiveness, life, and salvation as we believe his words and trust his promises.

READ "GROWING..." pages 145-147.

THINK about these statements and then write why they are true:

1. In the Lord's Supper God assures us personally of forgiveness.

2. Jesus gives us great blessings in the Lord's Supper.

3. The Holy Spirit is at work in the Lord's Supper to strengthen our faith and help us grow in the new life.

4. The power of the Lord's Supper lies in the words, "Given and shed for you for the forgiveness of sins".

TIME FOR REFLECTION

FIND texts or words from the Small Catechism on pages 145-147 of "Growing..." which tell how these people feel about the Sacrament.

a. Going to Holy Communion made Alan feel very thankful to Jesus for his love and forgiveness. "I must really try to live for Christ," he said to himself.

b. As Martin knelt at the altar and heard the words of Jesus, "This is my body and blood given and shed for you", he was quite sure that God had forgiven him.

c. The Holy Communion service helped Jane to stop worrying about her life and to be more contented. She felt at peace with God.

d. The pastor gave old Mrs. Charles Holy Communion as she lay sick in hospital. "I'm not afraid of dying," she told him. "I know that I will go to heaven to be with Jesus."

FOR DEVOTIONS

A "When the Word of God is joined with the bread and wine it becomes a sacrament." These words of St. Augustine teach us how God uses ordinary, familiar things like bread and wine in the Sacrament and connects them with the power of his holy Word to bring us his love and grace.

THINK about what Augustine says as you REPEAT part 3 of Holy Communion from the Small Catechism, "The Power of Holy Communion".

B READ John 6:35-40 and THINK about what it means for you that Jesus is the Bread of Life.
What special meaning does this have when you go to Holy Communion?

C COMPARE parts 2 and 3 of Holy Baptism and Holy Communion in the Small Catechism ("Growing..." pages 19 and 20).
Notice that you receive the same blessings in both sacraments.
Thank God that through the Lord's Supper he assures you that your sins are forgiven and that you have life and salvation.

FAMILY TIME

You could READ the words of Augustine (A above) to your family and DISCUSS with them what he means. READ John 6:35-40 and pray the Lord's Prayer together.

MORE TO DO

Use the code to work out these important words of Jesus.

Y /	V $
G #	A +
T ?	O (
U "	R =
N *	F)
D x	I @
S !	E %
H ¢	

@ $ % *   + * x   ! ¢ % x   ) (=

/ ("   ) (=   ? ¢ %   ) (= # @ $ % * % ! !

( )   ! @ * !

Write one or two sentences saying how you feel about Jesus' invitation to come to his Supper.

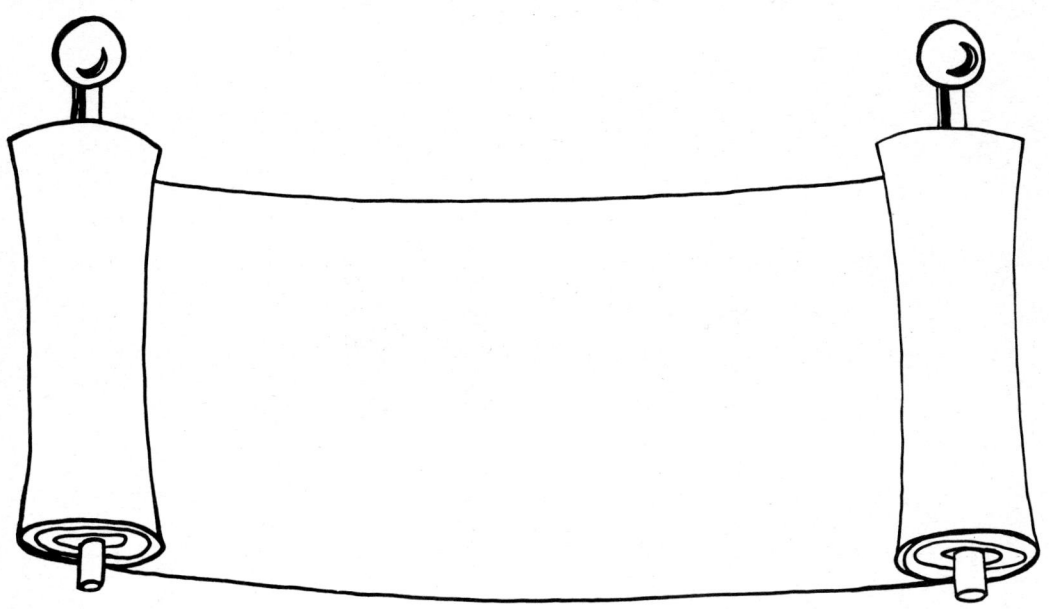

36 CHAPTER — READY FOR THE FEAST

Jesus' invitation to come to his feast must be taken seriously. We need to prepare ourselves so that we receive the Sacrament to the glory of God and for our blessing. We can't make ourselves worthy of this feast. But the Holy Spirit prepares us. He leads us to confess our sins and to believe that Jesus died for us so that we come in faith and receive help and strength to live as God's people.

READ "GROWING..." pages 149-151.

CHOOSE the best endings to complete these sentences:

1. Jesus invites us to his feast ....
2. The Holy Spirit prepares us for the Sacrament ....
3. We prepare ourselves outwardly ....
4. God tells us to examine ourselves ...
5. Only those who are repentant ....
6. Even if our faith is weak ....

a. ... in order to show respect for our Lord.
b. ... and believe Jesus' words should go to the Sacrament.
c. ... we should go to the Sacrament to be strengthened.
d. ... as he leads us to repentance.
e. ... even though we are sinners.
f. ... to see whether we are sorry for our sins, believe in Jesus, and intend to live a godly life.

TIME FOR REFLECTION

TICK the examples of people who are ready for the Sacrament. Then WRITE why.

a. John got good marks in a test because he had cheated. Rather than being sorry about his cheating he thought he was rather clever because he didn't get caught. He went to Holy Communion the next Sunday without thinking about what he had done.

b. Angela sometimes doubted whether Jesus' body and blood could really be present in the Lord's Supper, but she kept on going to the Sacrament and asked God to strengthen her faith.

c. Hal had a bad habit of telling lies. He often went to Holy Communion but didn't ask God to help him overcome his bad habit.

d. Beth didn't have any nice new clothes. But she didn't let that stop her going to the Lord's Supper because she wanted God's forgiveness and help to live a Christian life.

e. Andy bore a grudge against Ben. He went to Holy Communion even though he was planning to get his own back on Ben.

FOR DEVOTIONS

Dr. Martin Luther prepared some questions and answers especially to help people prepare to go to the Lord's Supper. THINK *about* them to discover their message for those who go to the Lord's Supper.

A *Are you sorry for your sins?* Yes, I am sorry I have sinned against God.

   What do you deserve from God because of your sins? I deserve that he should be angry with me and punish me with death and eternal damnation.

B *What has Christ done for you that you trust him?*
   He died for me and shed his blood for me on the cross for the forgiveness of sins.

   How do you know this?
   From the holy Gospel and from the words of Jesus in the Sacrament, and also by his body and blood which he gives me as his guarantee that I am forgiven.

C *Why do you want to go to the Sacrament?*
   So that I may become quite sure that Jesus died for my sin out of his great love for me, and learn from him to love God and my neighbour.

   Why should you receive the Sacrament often?
   Because of God's command and the promise Jesus makes to me, and to help me in my troubles.

READ Psalm 25:11-18. CONFESS your sins to God and thank him for his forgiveness.

FAMILY TIME

Members of your family who go to the Lord's Supper could TALK about how they prepare themselves for the Sacrament. You could have a family DISCUSSION on fasting and its value.
READ the section from "Growing...", "How Do We Get Ready For The Lord's Supper?" page 150. Conclude the devotion by reading or singing the hymn "I come to thee" (Lutheran Hymnal 320).

MORE TO DO

To find the three questions you can ask to prepare yourself for Holy Communion, fill the listed letters into the blank spaces directly above by rows. Use each letter only once. (You can help yourself by finding the three questions on page 150 of "Growing...".)

A	M																												
D	O		I		I	N	T	I	L	D	E	T	T	R	R	I	V	J	E	S	S	S	Y	O	D	S	D	C	H	O	L	D	M	E
D	M		I		R	E	A	E	N	V		S	O	H	L	Y		F	O	A	U	M	G	D	S	I	N	S	F	I	R
A	O		I		B	E	L	L	E	Y		O	A	T	E	R					I	E

UNIT SIX: THE CHURCH IN ACTION

37 HERE ARE THE KEYS!
CHAPTER

Jesus gave his church the power to forgive and to retain sins. This power, or authority, is called the "Office of the Keys". Heaven is opened to those who repent and is shut to those who will not repent. The church acts as Christ's representative when it uses this power and serves people with the Word and Sacraments. Pastors use the Office of the Keys publicly for Christian congregations. But all God's people are priests and are to use the Power of the Keys in their private lives.

READ "GROWING..." pages 153-155.
FIND answers to these questions:

1. What does it mean to remit and to retain sins?
2. How does your congregation use the Office of the Keys?
3. To whom did Jesus give the Office of the Keys?
4. What is the "office of the ministry" and what special work does God give to pastors.
5. What does it mean that all Christians are priests?

TIME FOR REFLECTION

THE CHURCH AT WORK

It was a happy day for the Hansen family. Baby Jamie was baptized that Sunday morning. The whole congregation shared the family's joy as Jamie's sins were washed away and God made him his child. In his sermon, Pastor Hudson challenged members of his congregation to be witnesses for Jesus. "What a privilege to be able to tell people who are worried about their sins that God forgives them for Jesus' sake!" he said. The pastor was pleased to see the church full that morning and that many attended the Lord's Supper.

After the service, Pastor Hudson spoke with the elders about two people who had stopped coming to church. "They are not sorry for what they are doing wrong," he told the elders. "We must pray for them lest they be lost to us." Several elders said they would visit these people and speak with them.

Later in the afternoon the pastor visited a man in hospital to give him Holy Communion. The man confessed his sins and the pastor assured him of God's forgiveness and gave him the Sacrament. On his way home he called on a widow who was worried about her son. "I keep warning him and asking him not to go out with this wild crowd," she said, "but he doesn't seem to listen". "Perhaps I can help by speaking to him," the pastor suggested.

Late that evening the pastor thought about the busy day he had spent. He was thankful for another day in which he had been able to work for his Lord.

UNDERLINE all the references in the story to the Office of the Keys.

FOR DEVOTIONS

A A Christian in the congregation at Corinth had committed a shameful sin and had not repented. Paul urged the other Christians in Corinth to use the Office of the Keys and exclude him from the congregation. But then this man repented.

How should the congregation now use the Office of the Keys?
READ 2 Corinthians 2:6-8, 10.
Whose representative was Paul when he forgave sins? Who forgives you as Christ's representative?

B Pastors are described in many different ways in the Bible. LOOK up these texts and find out how pastors are described and the work they are to do:

Matthew 4:19; 2 Corinthians 6:1; Jeremiah 23:4; 2 Timothy 2:3; Isaiah 52:7; 2 Corinthians 5:20; 1 Corinthians 4:1.

REPEAT the memory verse 1 Corinthians 4:1 and offer a prayer for your pastor, asking God to help and bless him in his work.

C When Admiral Foote was in Thailand he invited the king and his family to dinner on his ship. When his guests were seated at the table the Admiral said grace, asking God's blessing on the food. The king was surprised. "I thought only Christian missionaries asked a blessing," he said. "True," replied the Admiral, "but, you see, every Christian is a missionary!"

What did the Admiral mean? REPEAT the memory verse Mark 16:15 and THINK about how you can "preach the Gospel" to others.

FAMILY TIME

Have a family DISCUSSION about what it means that all Christians are priests. You could READ 1 Peter 2:9 and the section, "All Christians Are Priests" from "Growing..." page 155, and TALK about the statement "In private all Christians minister with the Gospel". Pray, asking God to help the family live as priests of Christ.

MORE TO DO

What unlocks the door of heaven? Decide on answers to the three questions below and then write the letters of the words on the key. (You can check the answers in Acts 16:31.)

1. Another way of saying that we must have <u>faith</u> in something.

   (2 words: 7 letters;   2 letters)

2. Someone who says he is the door.

   (3 words: 3 letters; 4 letters; 5 letters)

3. What will happen if you have fallen into the sea and hold on to a life-belt until a boat rescues you.

   (5 words: 3 letters; 3 letters; 4 letters;
              2 letters; 5 letters)

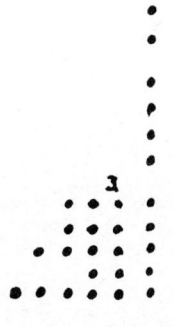

38 CHAPTER

I'M SORRY!

Admitting our sins to God and hearing his word of forgiveness is called "Confession". Because of our many sins we continually need to confess to God to be assured of forgiveness, or absolution. When we confess to God we tell him all our sins. However, when we are troubled by particular sins we can confess privately to the pastor and receive God's absolution personally. When we have done wrong to others we should ask their forgiveness.

READ "GROWING..." pages 157-159.

THINK about these questions and then WRITE in your answers.

1. Why is confession an important part of a Christian's life?

2. Why can we be sure of God's forgiveness?

3. What is the purpose of private confession?

4. Why should we apologise to those we have wronged?

TIME FOR REFLECTION

TICK the endings which describe God-pleasing attitudes. Cross out those that are wrong attitudes. (There may be more than one right ending.)

a. When you have fallen into sin, God wants you to feel:
   ... sure you will be punished because you are a Christian,
   ... sorry that you have offended God,
   ... sure that God forgives you for Jesus' sake.

b. Robert heard the pastor say in the service, "Your sins are forgiven you". God wants him to feel:
   ... uncertain whether God had forgiven him,
   ... doubtful whether the pastor had the right to forgive,
   ... sure of God's forgiveness.

c. Brenda had done something very wrong. As God's child she should:
   ... try to ignore what she had done and forget it,
   ... put off telling God about it till she felt better,
   ... confess to God what she had done.

d. When you confess your sins privately to the pastor you should feel:
   ... sure that you have received God's forgiveness personally,
   ... sorry that you worried the pastor,
   ... confident that the pastor will not tell others what you have confessed.

e. Jesus wants us to apologise to those we have wronged because:
   ... we can feel pleased with ourselves for owning up,
   ... it will help restore good relationships,
   ... it is the loving thing to do.

FOR DEVOTIONS

A Why do Christians keep on confessing their sins to God?
Consider this: if we don't think we're sick we won't take any medicine. If we don't believe the house is on fire we won't try to escape. Similarly, unless we realize we are hopelessly lost in sin we won't see our need of the Saviour. But when we do realize our guilt and helplessness we cry out for Christ to save us and praise God for the forgiveness and help he offers through him. By God's grace this will be our daily experience.

THINK about this as you READ 1 John 1:5-10.

B This story is really a parable. See if you can discover its deeper meaning.

A millionaire received some very good news which made him very happy. Looking out of his window he noticed a man walking past dressed in rags and looking miserable. "I'll make someone else happy, too," the millionaire thought. Taking some pieces of fine jewelry out of his safe, he went out to the street and offered the jewels to the beggar. But the beggar only scowled at him. "Why are you making a fool of me? I don't need your help," the poor man growled and walked off angrily. "How can you help someone who doesn't trust you?" the millionaire thought sadly as he walked back inside.

To help you understand what this story teaches about God's offer of forgiveness, *READ Acts 13:44-52.* Ask God to help you be thankful for his wonderful gift of forgiveness.

C *THINK about your life today. TELL God how you have failed and ASK him to forgive you.*

FAMILY TIME

Members of the family may wish to *TALK* about problems that arise in family life. They may wish to express sorrow for wrong that has been done and receive forgiveness. You could *READ 1 John 1:5-10* and the hymn, "Today thy mercy calls us" (Lutheran Hymnal 305).

MORE TO DO

Work out the maze. Begin at the arrow and move in one continuous line from each letter to the next in any direction, to spell out the text below. Dont't cross over your line at any time and use each letter only once.

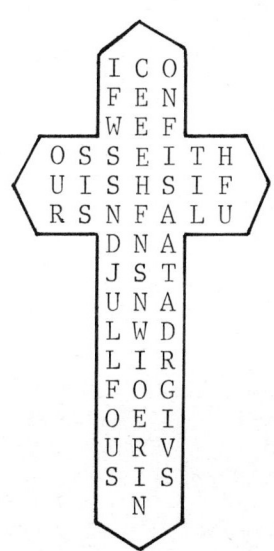

IF WE CONFESS OUR SINS, HE IS FAITHFUL AND
JUST AND WILL FORGIVE OUR SINS

39 CHAPTER
OUR LIFE OF WORSHIP

As God's people we aim to serve God and give him praise and thanks. This means that our whole life is worship as we live for God's glory. However, there are special times and places when we worship God together with our fellow Christians and in our private lives. As we worship God he blesses us through his Word and Sacraments and helps us live and grow as his people. We respond to God's grace in worship as we confess our faith and pray, praise and give thanks.

READ "GROWING..." pages 161-164.

COMPLETE the sentences by filling in the words:

Through his ..... God leads us to worship him. He comes to us in his .... and .... through which the .... works in us. We gladly .... by showing our .... and ...... to him. We join with the .... in worshipping God through the ...... on .... and other .... of the church .... . In the liturgy we ...... as God ...... to us; we ...... our faith and sing his .... We come to God with our .... and .... and share in his holy ..... We also worship God in our .... lives and in our .... day by day. Indeed, our whole .... is worship as we live for God's ..... .

(*life   liturgy   love   year   grace   speaks   Holy Spirit   sacraments   listen   congregation   respond   thanks   Word   prayers   glory   confess   praise   feast   private   Sundays   offerings   festivals   families*)

FOR DEVOTIONS

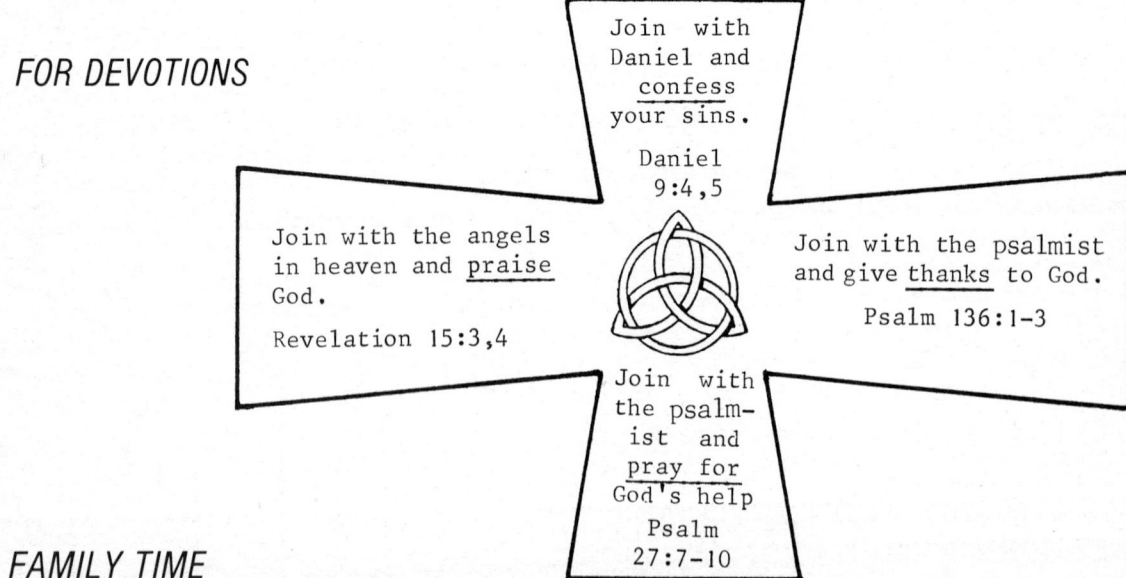

FAMILY TIME

SHOW your family the illustration of the liturgy on page 163 of "Growing..." and *DISCUSS* the order of service. Close by praising God in the words of Revelation 15:3,4.

CHAPTER 40 — KEEP ON GROWING

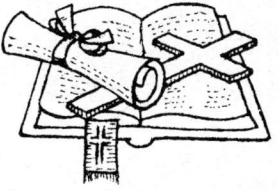

Ever since God made you his child through Holy Baptism you have been growing as one of his people. God has been with you as you have studied this course to bless you through his Word. Now you are looking forward to the day of your confirmation. At that service you will confess your faith and ask God to bless you so that you may be one of his people throughout your life and forever. As you share in the life and work of God's family you can be sure that God will help you to keep on growing through his Word and Sacraments. With his blessing you can lead a full and active life as a member of his church on earth until he takes you to your heavenly home.

FAMILY TIME

TALK to your family about the meaning of confirmation and how your family will prepare for the day of your confirmation. READ or sing the hymn "My Maker be thou nigh" (Lutheran Hymnal 296).

REVIEW THE SIX CHIEF PARTS OF CHRISTIAN DOCTRINE.
Work out the exercises and then write a short response to each section.

1. READ the Ten Commandments in the Small Catechism ("Growing..." page 17).

    DECODE the message to find the key to understanding the Ten Commandments. (Key to morse code is on p.11.)

    ```
    -.-- --- ..-     ... .... .- .-.. .-..

    .-.. --- ...- .    --. --- -..    .-- .. - ....

    .- .-.. .-..    -.-- --- ..- .-.

    .... . .- .-. -    .- -. -..    -.-- --- ..- .-.

    -. .. --. .... -... --- ..- .-.    .- ...

    -.-- --- ..- .-. ... . .-.. ..-.
    ```

    Ask God to help you grow in knowing and doing his will:

2. READ the three articles of the Creed in the Small Catechism ("Growing..." p.18).
    LOOK UP the texts and write in the name given to the Lord and what he has done.

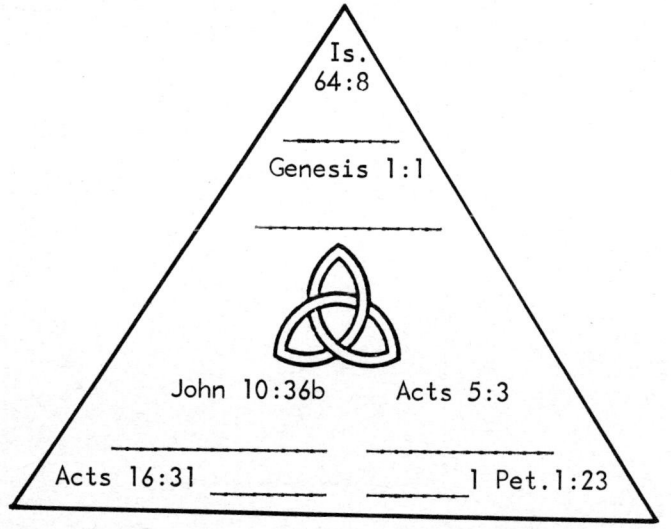

Thank the Triune God for all he has done for you:

3. READ the explanation of the Lord's Prayer ("Growing..." p. 18,19).

REVIEW the Lord's Prayer as you answer the questions:

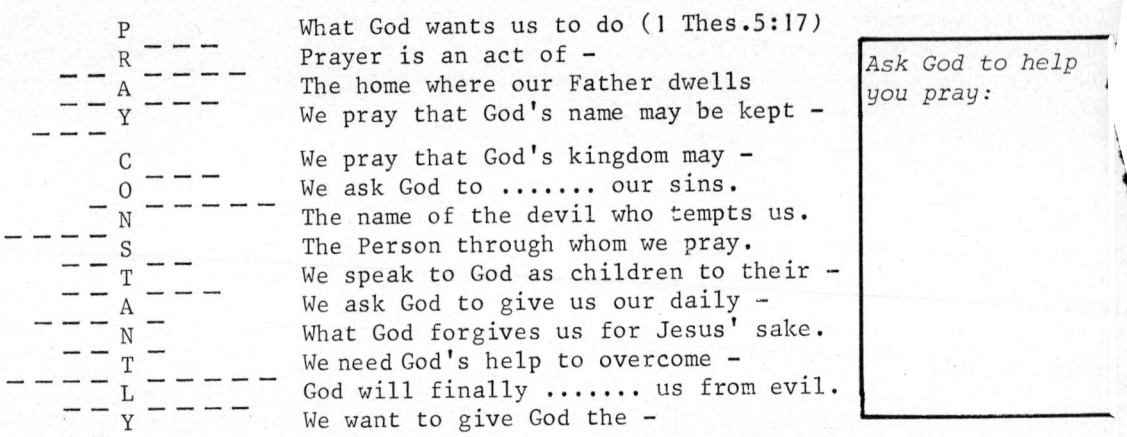

Ask God to help you pray:

4. READ the explanation of Holy Baptism ("Growing..." p. 19).
DECODE the message to discover God's promise.
(Numbers stand for letters of the alphabet.)

8 5   23 8 15   2 5 12 9 5 22 5 19

1 14 4   9 19   2 1 16 20 9 26 5 4

23 9 12 12   2 5   19 1 22 5 4

Ask God to help you live as his baptized child:

5. READ the explanation of Holy Communion ("Growing..." p. 20).
THINK about Jesus' invitation to his Supper as you fit the words onto the altar.

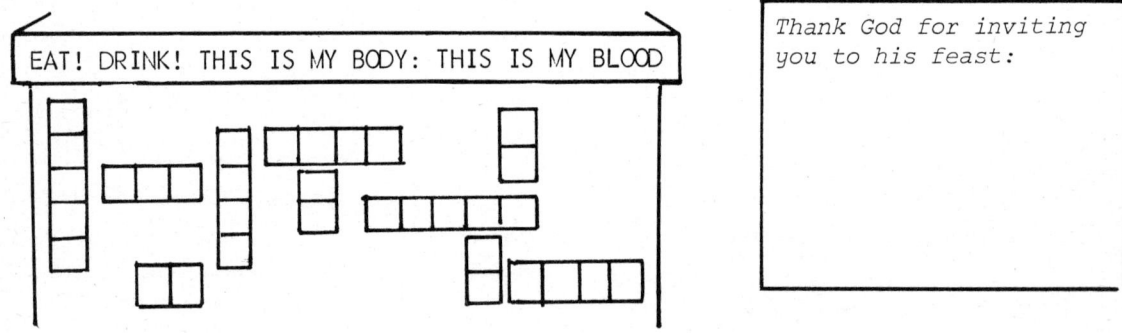

EAT! DRINK! THIS IS MY BODY: THIS IS MY BLOOD

Thank God for inviting you to his feast:

6. READ the Office of the Keys and Confession ("Growing... p. 20).
WORK OUT the key to finding the text. Then learn the text by heart.

The first letter of the first word in each of these texts: (use RSV Bible).

John 20:21;   Luke 5:17;   Mark 6:1;
Matt. 16:13;

The numbers mentioned in these texts
Ezekiel 4:10;   Judges 10:2.

Ask God to help you be his witness: